This is a book about how to transform hospitality—a rare commodity, even in our Christian circles—into something heavenly. As someone who has stayed in the Janssen home, I can say that Jo Ann lives out what she has written!

BROTHER ANDREW
Author, *God's Smuggler*

If my friend Jo Ann Janssen was a hobbit, she would be serving the perfect cup of tea in a cozy corner of Bag End while we guests enjoyed a good chat by a warm fire. In *Heavenly Hospitality,* Jo helps us turn the glossy magazine fantasy of hospitality into a practical, inviting reality.

KURT BRUNER
Author, *Finding God in the Lord of the Rings*

Appendices, time lines, and tips galore make this one of the most useful books on hospitality ever written. You'll want to keep it nearby for ready reference when planning a bridal shower or trying to figure out how much roast beef each of your guests will need to feel satisfied. It's all there sandwiched (pun intended) between the covers of *Heavenly Hospitality.*

GWEN ELLIS
Owner, Seaside Creative Services
Port Hueneme, California

From Jo Ann I've learned how simple and rewarding hospitality can be. Her chatty but informative book is all you'll ever need to make guests feel comfortable in staying for five minutes or five days.

LISSA HALLS JOHNSON
Author, *Stuck in the Sky* and *The Worst Wish*

Jo Ann's love for guests and her gift of hospitality shine on every page in this lovely book. With practical advice and thought-provoking insights, she encourages even the most timid hostess to celebrate with grace the next time company comes calling.

ROBIN JONES GUNN
Best-selling author of the Sisterchicks™ novels and *Tea at Glenbrooke*

I need this book desperately! I am what you would call hospitality challenged. Jo Ann Janssen's book is just the resource I want to keep handy for those times when my desire to serve supersedes my innate giftedness, or lack thereof.

LISA WHELCHEL
Author, *The Facts of Life and Other Lessons My Father Taught Me* and *Creative Correction;* Founder, MomTime Ministries

Jo Ann has captured the essence of what true hospitality means—and without the guilt! She shows you how to cheerfully and easily share your heart and home no matter what your situation.

JONNI MCCOY
Author, founder of Miserly Moms

FOCUS ON THE FAMILY® PRESENTS

Heavenly Hospitality

250+ everyday ideas
for welcoming guests
into your home

Jo Ann Janssen

Tyndale House Publishers, Inc. ‣ Wheaton, IL

Visit Tyndale's exciting Web site at www.tyndale.com

Edited by Kimberly Miller

Designed by Jacqueline L. Noe

Library of Congress Cataloging-in-Publication Data

Janssen, Jo Ann
   Heavenly hospitality : 250+ everyday ideas for welcoming guests into your home / Jo Ann Janssen.
     p. cm.
   Includes bibliographical references.
   ISBN 0-8423-8105-8 (sc)
   1. Entertaining. 2. Hospitality. I. Title.
   TX731.J364 2004
   642'.4—dc22
                                                2004001061

Printed in the United States of America

08 07 06 05 04
5   4   3   2   1

Dedication

I dedicate this book to my husband, Al, who personifies hospitality; to my daughter, Anna, who is becoming a very competent, selfless, and gracious hostess; to my son Jon, who generously invites his buddies for dinner or to spend the night and tells me as they come in the door; and to my eldest, Josh, who has grown to be a confident and sensitive host. I am one proud mother!

Contents

Acknowledgments

I want to thank three talented and encouraging women at Tyndale: Jan Long Harris, who believed in my project in the first place; Barbara Kois, whose title of product development manager only scrapes the surface of all she does; and Kimberly Miller, who took my raw material and tactfully organized it into something useful and accessible for my readers.

I would not even have attempted to write a book without the prayers and encouragement of many people, especially my Bible study friends, the praying women in my Moms in Touch group, many loyal people in my church, and my dear friend, Vickie Howard. They all understood that I would have to cut down on practicing hospitality so I could write about it. During the writing of this book I had to have foot surgery, my mother-in-law passed away, my three children were going through life-stage changes, and quite a few friends and family members came through town and stayed at our home. It was a busy time of life. My friends were with me all the way. I appreciated all their hospitality during that time.

All through this book I point to the influence of my parents, Chuck and Dorothy Pulsipher. I often thank God for the example of their priorities and generous spirit, which continues with their four kids and nine grandkids who are now carrying on the family traditions. I pray that my readers will begin the kind of hospitable lifestyle that I grew up with, so that their children can carry it on as well.

We've been duped. Yep. Conned by editors of glossy magazines into equating hospitality with exotic gourmet feasts served in extravagantly decorated dining rooms. Since we quickly realize that those articles and their fancy photos set up a standard that is impossible to meet, we figure we're off the hook, right? Wrong!

It is time to dispel the magazine myth of hospitality and get back to biblical basics. The Bible is full of reminders to open our homes and our hearts to others. God told the Israelites not to harvest all of the grain in their fields but to leave some for the poor and the foreigners, treating them kindly as they would have liked to have been treated when they lived as foreigners in Egypt. Several times in their letters, the apostles Paul, Peter, and John encouraged the early believers—who often lived in extreme poverty—to invite folks into their humble homes. Of course, those letters were written for us too. Just after the apostle Peter says to "love each other deeply," he reminds believers to "offer hospitality to one another without grumbling" (1 Peter 4:8-9).

The key to being hospitable, then, is grounded in loving others rather than owning and showing off an exquisite, perfectly decorated house. What exactly does it mean to be hospitable? The Merriam-Webster dictionary defines it as being, "friendly, kind, and solicitous towards guests." I would add that it involves being sensitive to those who are needy, initiating invitations and obeying God when he urges you to reach out to someone.

Our home, which really belongs to God,

can be a conduit of blessings to many. Our living room may be the most comfortable location to hold a Moms in Touch meeting. The kitchen table may be the ideal location to sit with our friend after she's just been told she has cancer. By getting our minds off our shortcomings and ourselves we are free to help others.

This book is not a set of hard-and-fast rules to follow with recipes requiring a gourmet kitchen. It is about how the Janssen Five (that's my family!), in our modest, nondescript home on Nevermind Lane, have learned to follow God's leading in opening our home and the practical lessons we have learned that make it easier every time.

First we'll take an honest look at the very real pressures that may be preventing you from opening your home to others. We'll also discuss why it is worth making the time and effort to practice hospitality. And if you've ever been tempted to hide in your coat closet when the doorbell rings, you may benefit from my tips on making your home ready for friends who may show up unexpectedly.

Once your heart and home are ready, you can begin trying out the hundreds of hospitality ideas presented in this book. Many are quite simple; others may be most appropriate only when you have lots of time (or ambition!). The appendices provide reproducible planning lists that you can use whenever you plan a dinner party, birthday party, or shower.

The Janssen Five relish just about every aspect of opening up our home (housecleaning being the one drawback). I attribute it to my rich heritage. Growing up as a preacher's kid (and grandkid), hospitality was an integral part of life. Visitors to our small church were invited to Sunday dinner in our home. Counseling occurred around our dining room table on weeknights. A cup of coffee or a glass of cold water was offered to all who stopped by for "a short visit."

Perhaps you don't share my rich background. You may find the whole concept of hospitality frightening or overwhelming. What will people think of our humble home and bumbling attempts? Who has time for guests with all the housekeeping, carpooling, and outside commitments at church, our kids' schools, and possibly to our employer? Yet God makes it very clear in his Word that we are to practice hospitality, have a servant's heart, and give generously of ourselves and our resources.

The more you practice hospitality, the more comfortable you will become. After a while you will realize that most people are thrilled that someone invited them over. No one has judged your décor or cooking! When you do not mention the stain on your sofa, nobody else notices it, either. As you begin to get your mind off yourself and concentrate on others, you will learn to savor the joys of hospitality—not to impress, but to bless!

"Business! . . . Mankind was my business. The common welfare was my business; charity, mercy, forebearance, and benevolence were all my business. The dealings of my trade were but a drop of water in the comprehensive ocean of my business!"

—Marley's ghost to Scrooge,
A Christmas Carol by Charles Dickens

Chapter 1
Hospitality—Why Bother?

Elly Parker grudgingly opened her tired eyes to glare at the alarm clock. 6:30 A.M. She had just fallen into a deep, dreamless sleep when that annoying buzzer beckoned her to get up. A good night's rest had eluded her as she worried about the day to come. This was the day the pastor and his family were coming for dinner, and Elly wanted to impress them.

Instead of sleeping Elly had tossed around dinner menu options. She had never had anyone over for dinner before but according to the magazines she read, fancy foods were expected. She felt that all her usual family favorites were too humble. Something showy and expensive had to be prepared. But what? While watching TV the night before she had thumbed through her cookbooks. Everything looked so difficult, expensive, complicated, and time consuming.

Besides the menu, other concerns kept her awake. When would she find time

to clean the house, do the grocery shopping, set the table, and cook dinner with all the other commitments she had? Could she get out of driving for the fourth-grade fall field trip at the last moment? Was there time to buy new dishes? Could her budget handle all the costly foods *and* new dishes?

Twelve hours later Pastor Sam Schubert, his wife, Sally, and their two toddlers arrived a fashionable five minutes late. Elly's long-suffering husband, Paul, welcomed them at the front door and invited them to sit in the living room. The room smelled like it had just been vacuumed and indeed the vacuum cleaner was still warm. Paul offered their guests soft drinks. They accepted. Paul went to the kitchen to fetch them. There he found his bedraggled Elly up to her elbows in strange salad dressing ingredients amid three open cookbooks and piles of dirty dishes. It didn't look like dinner would be served any time soon.

Paul valiantly returned to the Schuberts to try to keep them entertained until dinner. Conversation canvassed everything from Creation to conservation to conservatives. Elly would have enjoyed it if she hadn't been struggling in the kitchen to get the new food processor running. The Parker kids played with the visiting toddlers who soon became hungry and restless.

Sally eventually popped into the kitchen to see if she could help. Elly firmly denied any need of assistance. Sally wondered what had come over her usually placid friend and felt it safest to leave her alone.

Ninety minutes passed before dinner was announced. The hungry mob was in the mood to eat just about anything, but after grace Elly's kids loudly questioned the identity of the suspicious green unlettucey-looking stuff in the salad. The pastor's toddlers followed suit and refused to eat it. The basket of hard rolls emptied fast.

The ensuing dinner presentation would have made any professional cook proud. The standing rib roast majestically stood amid a wreath of parsley. The asparagus, though cold, was attractively arranged with swirls of yellow sauce on top. Exotic spices made the potatoes out-of-this-world delicious— to a discerning, sophisticated palate. Unfortunately, the table was surrounded with regular folks.

During the meal poor Elly constantly rushed between the dining room and kitchen. She hardly had a minute to enjoy the fruits of her labor much less the pleasure of visiting with her company. Besides that, she seemed angry, mumbling things like, "I have to do everything around here," and "Can't Paul see that I need help?" The tone of the evening became strained at best.

When one of her kids accidentally spilled his drink, Elly came unglued. Her freshly ironed tablecloth was a mess! Why couldn't he be more careful! Her son stood in the corner for fifteen minutes as punishment. Everyone was embarrassed—not by the spilled milk but by Elly's overreaction. The ambiance took another dive.

Using toddler bedtimes as an excuse, the pastor and his family left as soon as the last bite of rich dessert was gone. They seemed glad to leave. Sally told Elly that she would like to get together with her again sometime. Perhaps a coffee-shop date?

As soon as the door closed behind the Schuberts Elly buried her head on Paul's broad shoulders and had a good cry. The evening had been a disaster! What would they think of her?! She was a failure! How could she ever show her face at church again? It was quite a pity party. Paul just held her and prayed. He knew Elly would be more objective and teachable after a good night's rest.

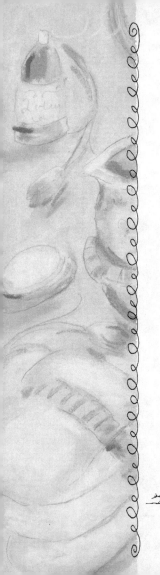

Elly had a lot to learn about hospitality. The Schuberts didn't make a quick exit because they didn't like the asparagus dish. They left because they felt like an inconvenience to their hostess. Elly stumbled because her mind-set was out of kilter with the mission of hospitality.

We shouldn't be too quick to judge Elly, however. Like her, many of us rarely invite others into our homes because we are so busy with other responsibilities. When we do extend an invitation, we are often plagued with the same doubts and insecurities that kept Elly awake all night.

So before we even venture into the "how-to's" of hospitality, we need to address the basic question: Why bother? We'll do this by considering seven key questions.

WHY SHOULD I SHARE?
Everything belongs to God.
Psalm 24:1 says, "The earth is the Lord's, and everything in it, the world, and all who live in it." Colossians 1:16 adds that "all things were created by him and for him." Without the Creator you would have nothing. Any good blessing you can mention is a gift from God for you to use for his purposes. This includes your home, the food in your fridge, and your time. Yes, you get to use them, but in truth you are merely a steward of his good gifts. How are you using your God-given home?

Many Christians have a dedication ceremony when they move into their new home. At ours we recognized that our modest "fixer-upper," like everything else we own, in reality belongs to God and is to be used for furthering his kingdom. Your home isn't just where you unwind at the end of a long day; it is a gift from God meant to be used for his service. Viewing it with that attitude can transform how you use your home.

God has richly blessed you for a reason. Other people are that reason. Once you accept that, you'll begin thinking how you can use your home to reach out to others. The extra bedroom becomes "The Missionary Room." You arrange your living room furniture so that it is conducive for conversation because you want to be able to comfortably listen to and pray for a hurting friend. You move the china cabinet into the living room so you can fit a larger table into the dining room where more people can be seated. You choose carpet based on how well it hides dirt rather than its color or texture. (You will find more specific help for making your home hospitality-friendly in chapter 2.)

I often hear people say that they do not have time to practice hospitality. They are really saying that it is not a priority. Loving and caring for others is mentioned—perhaps

I should say commanded—so often in Scripture that opportunities to do so should be on our mind constantly. Often the biggest obstacle to obedience is our to-do list, which is generally filled with a list of tasks rather than the names of people. Many of those things could wait another day while you minister to the people God has put in your life today. Better yet, put hospitality on your to-do list.

WHY SHOULD I CARE?
People have eternal value.
Eternity will be spent with *whos,* not *whats.*
People have eternal value. Things do not.

‿‿‿‿‿‿‿‿‿‿ *Reality Check* ‿‿‿‿‿‿‿‿‿‿

- Whatever you have is good enough.
- Your furniture does not have to match, look nice, or be new.
- Your attitude is what is important. Welcome all visitors with a smile, open heart, and generous soul. That is what they will remember.

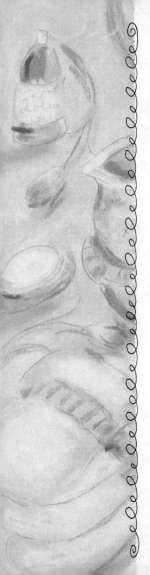

In 2 Corinthians 5:15-16, Paul reminds us that Christ "died for all, that those who live should no longer live for themselves but for him who died for them and was raised again. *So from now on we regard no one from a worldly point of view*" (italics mine).

I receive much more joy from my relationships than I ever will from my stuff. When I count my blessings, they all have a first and last name. My fondest memories all revolve around loved ones, and many of the best are times when I opened my home to bless others, only to find myself abundantly blessed by my guests.

Last year some friends from Oregon spent a few days at the Janssen B & B. We wanted to give them a lovely time because we knew that they had been experiencing some difficulties in their marriage. Also, we were aware that one of their children had spent the last ten years struggling with depression. While they were with us, our friends immediately recognized the symptoms of depression in one of our own children, who was going through a difficult time. They were able to counsel and encourage us. It was obvious that God had put them in our lives just when we needed them.

Quite often we can use our homes to meet the needs of people and practice hospitality. By the way, when Jesus told us to be hospitable, he didn't say we should wait until our living room furniture matches so we won't be embarrassed. That leads me to the next principle.

WHAT IF MY HOUSE ISN'T PERFECT?
Be content.
"Be content with such things as ye have" (Hebrews 13:5, KJV). Whether you live in a cozy cave or a crumbling castle, God has put you there right now, doing his ministry with what he has provided. The apostle Paul received guests while he was in prison. We should never be embarrassed by our homes.

Look at your home through the eyes of ministering instead of comparing it to the pictures in glossy decorating magazines. The family you invite for Sunday dinner will not care if they sit on unmatched chairs and eat off a variety of cheap dishes. They will just be tickled that someone actually had them over for a meal!

My grandma Pulsipher lived the last fifteen years of her long life in a single-wide mobile home. She welcomed many into her cozy place for coffee and counseling. I remember drinking tea served in china cups at her tiny table. She never apologized for her humble home—she just kept ministering.

Practicing contentment frees us up to do more important things. Which has greater eternal value: shopping for the perfect rug or hosting a Bible study in your home? It requires a great deal of time, energy, and money to keep up with the Joneses.

Are you content with your home or do you rearrange numbers until you can barely qualify for a bigger mortgage and nicer digs? I know a few people who live in posh neighborhoods but have gone into serious credit card debt because their house payment takes up so much of their monthly income. The financial pressure creates family discord, and the hopelessness of the situation is constantly on their minds. Their luxurious master bedroom is no longer conducive to sleep. Great house. Crummy life.

Right now much of my family's money is designated for educating our three children. That leaves very little for accumulating bigger and better things, but we always find a way to practice hospitality. Our values and contentment foster creativity.

WHAT IF I DON'T HAVE MUCH MONEY TO ENTERTAIN OTHERS?

Make the most of what you do have.

Jesus served five thousand men, along with an untold number of women and children, with a few loaves of bread and fishes. You may not be able to perform that miracle, but you may be surprised at what you can do if you get creative. In chapter 4 I will show you how to expand a typical family dinner to accommodate an extra guest or two.

You may think you simply do not have the right dishes, decorations, etc., to have dinner guests. Be content with what God has given you and look at what you do have through new eyes. Sheets for a tablecloth, wildflowers for a centerpiece, a set of mismatched teacups, and eating on a blanket in the middle of the living room floor can all be quite charming. I still remember when friends invited Al and me over to test a new recipe and ran out of dinner napkins. We cheerfully used kitchen towels instead.

My in-laws owned beautiful silver and gold flatware, an amazing array of hand-embroidered table linens, and lovely china. But they never used them. My husband had never even seen them until his mother gave them to me as gifts. Al's parents rarely entertained and when they did, they did not want to bother getting out the dishes and silverware. I want to encourage you to use those family heirlooms and wedding presents. Serving macaroni and cheese on china elevates the mundane to elegant.

Candlelight creates a special ambiance no matter what the rest of the environment looks like. A few dried flowers in a jam jar make a centerpiece. Coffee mugs can be used for soup bowls. An unmatched set of chairs, dishes, glasses, flatware, or napkins is so much more interesting than a perfectly coordinated one.

When you decide to serve pizza because

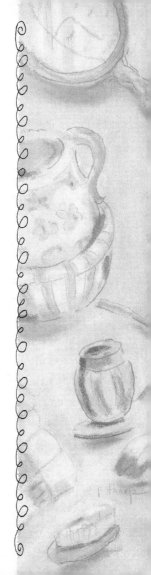

you would not have enough forks to go around if you served anything else, it pays to have a sense of humor. That brings me to my next point.

WHAT IF MY PARTY DOESN'T GO PERFECTLY?
Rejoice evermore!
The Bible tells us how to react to anything life brings us: "Rejoice evermore. . . . In every thing give thanks" (1 Thessalonians 5:16, 18, KJV). Have a sense of humor. Things will go wrong. You will forget your best friend's name, ruin dinner, have plumbing problems, and so on (just hopefully not all on the same evening!). The best reaction to life's little disasters is to laugh. It lightens up the atmosphere. It creates a memorable moment. It proves that you are humble and imperfect but that's okay with you.

One of our funniest memories is the time our oven caught fire. One fall Saturday after-noon Al was at home helping a professional baseball player and his wife plan the book they were to write. I had decided to put together a lasagna dinner that evening to cap off the day of work. Instead I woke up feeling awful. I called my neighborhood Italian restaurant and ordered lasagna, salad, and bread sticks. When it came to dessert, I figured I had enough energy to make my favorite carrot cake.

Have you ever noticed that many recipes give special instructions for those living in high altitudes? My family lives in Colorado so those instructions apply to me. Unfortunately, I had not baked this recipe since moving to my new mile-high home and forgot to make any adjust-ments. Consequently, the cake overflowed rather dramatically. I was able to rescue the cake by topping it with a generous amount of cream cheese frosting. But the oven was a mess.

I didn't think too much about the oven until it was time to heat up the lasagna I had picked up. First I preheated the oven, of course. When

I opened the oven door to slip in the lasagna,
I was greeted with flames—big, scorching, scary
flames. To make the occasion even more interesting, Al and our guests were standing right
there, with front-row seats to the impressive
conflagration. Without meaning to, I certainly
impressed and entertained my guests!

The flames subsided once I closed the oven
door but that didn't solve the problem of how
to heat up dinner. I phoned my next-door neighbor and explained the situation. She was glad to
lend me her oven, but she did want something in
return—the autograph of our well-known guest.
He agreed, probably motivated by hunger.

Actually we were all getting a bit famished
so we ate the salad and bread sticks to tide us
over. We were just finishing our salads when
my neighbor appeared with the lasagna. *That
didn't take very long to be warmed up,* I thought
to myself.

Well, it wasn't. My neighbor just could not

wait another minute to meet our guests and get
the promised autograph. After she left we ate
the lukewarm lasagna and laughed. What else
could we do?

We still laugh at the memory of amusing
our major league friends with the oven fire.
I could not have planned a more memorable
and hilarious time if I had tried!

What's in it for me?
It really is more blessed to give than to receive.
So far we've concentrated on how others benefit
from our hospitality. However, we also gain
when we obey the call to hospitality. Jesus'
words hardly need explaining: "When you give
a luncheon or dinner, do not invite your friends,
your brothers or relatives, or your rich neighbors; if you do, they may invite you back and so
you will be repaid. But when you give a banquet,
invite the poor, the crippled, the lame, the blind,
and you will be blessed. Although they cannot

repay you, you will be repaid at the resurrection of the righteous" (Luke 14:12-14). Jesus also said, "Give, and it will be given to you. A good measure, pressed down, shaken together and running over, will be poured into your lap. For with the measure you use, it will be measured to you" (Luke 6:38). How's that for a return on your investment?

One night I asked my family what benefits they think our family has gained by practicing hospitality. My son Josh said it is a great way to spend quality time with friends. My husband, Al, mentioned that a meal with guests is usually bigger and better, and the leftovers are good too! Anna, my daughter, thinks it is fun to meet new people.

Al and I agree that we have deeper and more meaningful friendships because we have invested the time it takes to build those relationships. Our growing circle of friends includes many people to whom we might not have natu-rally reached out to except for our desire to obey that still, small voice of God. Our views and understanding of the world have expanded because our guests have shared their varied lives with us. Our compassion for others has grown as we understand the tough situations others live in.

Although we have not seen much of the world, individuals from all corners have brought their piece of the world to us. Because of them we have insights into the difficult lives of our persecuted brothers and sisters in Christ all over the world. Their stories of family, culture, and community have broadened our experiences. We feel more connected to our global Christian family. There is no telling how this has influenced our impressionable children over the years.

By inviting people into our homes we have gotten our minds off ourselves (an unhealthy place to dwell, anyway) and onto the needs of others. This simple Christian concept has side

benefits. It combats loneliness. It puts our lives in perspective. And we end up feeling better for having done the right thing.

Like many Coloradans, we live hundreds of miles from relatives. To fill in for them we invite a houseful for holidays. The friendly mix creates a festive holiday mood. We can play more games, feast on different foods, and just have more fun when our home bursts at the seams with friends.

Hospitality has provided a creative outlet for the whole family. My daughter loves to decorate for her thematic birthday parties. Designing and making the decorations on a budget stretches her. All my children have been called upon to entertain the children of guests. Some of those tots require a lot of quick, creative thinking to keep them occupied. Coming up with last-minute centerpieces, adequate seating, recipe substitutions, and stretching meals call up all my creative juices.

Probably the greatest benefit Al and I have seen is the growth of our children. No, they haven't always handled every situation perfectly, but all three have learned well the fine art of being hosts and hostesses. They now think of others' needs before their own. Their manners constantly improve. Their world continues to expand as they discover a broader set of interests than their usual circle of friends provides.

Watching my kids in action when their friends are in our home warms my heart and thrills my soul. I've seen Jonathan sacrificially give up the last chocolate chip cookie. Anna has conscientiously watched to ensure all twelve of her party guests feel included. Joshua has given up his seat and offered a beverage to a late arrival without prompting. Yes, I am one proud mom.

WHAT'S THE BOTTOM LINE?
Remember, it is not about you.
It is not about how well you can cook. It is not

about how well decorated or how large your home is. It is not about how well the event goes or how impressed your guests are.

It is not about earning God's approval. It is an opportunity to bless others and honor God through the process of offering hospitality.

"If it weren't for the last minute, nothing would get done."

—ANONYMOUS

Chapter 2
Organization 101: Preparing Your Home for Guests

Remember Elly? Shortly before that fateful dinner at her home, she had come to realize that her home belonged to the Lord but that she hadn't been using it in that way. She had decided then to discover ways to use it to demonstrate Christ's love to others. She wanted her friends to feel free to stop by when they were having a tough day and for her children to be able to invite their friends over after school. She wanted to show her pastor and his family how much they were appreciated. That, in fact, was why she asked them to come for dinner.

So what went wrong? While Elly invited Sam and Sally Schubert over with the best of motives and intentions, panic set in when the day of the dinner came and she realized neither she nor

her home were ready for guests. She was, to put it simply, frantic and frazzled.

In contrast to Elly, I have never seen my mother the least bit frazzled—although I know my three siblings and I tried as hard as we could to accomplish that when we were growing up! Mom kept her table linens ironed, planned meals a week in advance, and thoroughly cleaned the house weekly. She kept the house picked up throughout the day. She made lists. She was *organized!* From her I learned the value of doing as much as I can as far ahead as possible.

This chapter is designed to help you get a grip on organizing your schedule and your home in such a way as to make it more compatible for hospitality. No, you will not have to invest in a mahogany dining room table that seats twelve. Instead I will give you ideas on how to creatively make the most of what you have. Before we get into rearranging your furniture, let us look at how to rearrange your schedule. We will begin with what I learned from my mother.

Do as much as you can as far ahead as you can.

This one principle will give you more peace of mind than you could ever imagine. You may not end up as unflappable as my mom, but you will feel a lot less stress. Working ahead will give you some leeway because something inevitably will go wrong. Your schedule will be interrupted when Johnny breaks his arm, your sink clogs, or your cake overflows all over the oven. Nothing ever goes according to plan. That is normal life. Think of Job 17:11: "My days have passed, my plans are shattered, and so are the desires of my heart." (Read the rest of Job to really put your worst day in perspective!)

I remember the Wednesday several years ago when my folks called to inform me of a change in plans: they would be arriving the next day in time for dinner, instead of Friday as previously mentioned. I am always delighted to have my parents visit, but I had already arranged with a friend to finish wallpapering my kitchen that Thursday.

My Crock-Pot came to the rescue. Before my friend Mitsy arrived I filled it with ingredients for beef stew and found a place in the family room, out of the way of the day's project, to plug it in. By the time my parents arrived, the kitchen was beautiful, my home smelled heavenly, and dinner was ready.

You can do so much ahead of time. Your Crock-Pot and freezer are your friends. Appendices A–D are designed to help you begin determining what to do and when as you plan parties and showers. Copy them. Use them. If you're planning a smaller event, take a few minutes to decide what needs to be done and the best time to do it.

Have a plan.

One of my friends complains that she has three calendars and still cannot get organized! Keep *one* master planner or calendar. Get organized with daily and weekly to-do lists. You may not always get everything done but a master list can bring order to your life. I have been known to add things to my list just so I can have the satisfaction of marking them off! You may want an extra organizational tool for planning big events. I use a notebook.

Plan your meals for the week. While preaching to the five thousand the entire morning, Jesus knew ahead of time what was being served for lunch! Jesus was cool and confident; his disciples were freaking out. That is what happens when you do not have a plan.

Now that my children are beyond the happy-with-hotdogs-every-night stage, they often help me make my meal plans. Sometimes we discuss them the day before I go grocery

shopping. I try to make sure everyone gets a say. Jon hates the black bean soup that is Anna's favorite, so if that is on the list, Jon gets to choose one of his favorites for another day or I serve it on a day when I know Jon won't be home. I encourage menus that reflect what is in season, what is in the freezer and fridge, and what is on sale. Chef's surprise and leftovers are often part of the plan. We also plan menus for any night when company is expected.

There are two main benefits to meal planning. It saves money and it prevents stress. I hate making dinner menu decisions when I am tired and hungry, which pretty well describes me at 4 P.M. when the kids ask what is for dinner.

You also will benefit from using housekeeping routines. See page 20 of this chapter for ideas on why and how to start these routines.

Delegate, delegate, delegate.

Get help. It is good to humbly admit you cannot do it all. Even Jesus put the disciples to work. Hand lists to your spouse and children. Before my kids could read, I gave them a pictorial list. They loved being productive. Throughout this book I will give you ideas of how you can constructively put almost every family member to work.

I also am in favor of enlisting the help of my guests. Both old friends and new enjoy the comfortable camaraderie it creates. It is so easy to talk and get to know someone while working together. A well-known author and her husband once arrived at my home thirty minutes early for a huge dinner party. I put them to work wiping down the deck furniture so we could expand the party to the great outdoors. They knew they were early and cheerfully went to work.

Communicate, communicate, communicate.
Talk to God. Discuss plans with your family. Be up front with your guests. It prevents so many misunderstandings.

I have had houseguests with indefinite departure times; dinner guests allergic to my main dish; smokers needing a place to light up; potluck attendees who arrived with a bag of lettuce for their "salad" but no serving utensils, dish, or dressing; and children in need of amusement. Better communication would have prevented those uncomfortable situations. Although both host and guest share in the responsibility of imparting pertinent facts, I think the host should initiate the process. Ask questions. Get specific information. While you probably won't want—or need—to cover all these details each time you extend an invitation, decide which of the following should be discussed in advance:

- Dinner guests' allergies, diet restrictions, and dislikes.
- If a guest is bringing part of a meal, be specific about amounts, food allergies, and diets. Some hostesses even send specific recipes to avoid confusion. Find out if they need oven, fridge, or freezer space so you will be ready.
- Guests' arrival and departure times.
- Dress code if applicable.
- Smoking or nonsmoking expectations.
- Number of guests expected.
- Special needs of those in wheelchairs, asthmatics, diabetics, etc.
- Any other expectations from either side.

These basic principles are foundational if you are serious about opening your home to others. The rest of the book contains practical ideas on making hospitality a part of your lifestyle and extending hospitality to others.

MAKING YOUR HOME WELCOMING FOR GUESTS

Although the only requirement for practicing hospitality is an open, obedient heart, you are more likely to feel comfortable inviting guests into your home if your home is generally orderly and clean. Following regular house-keeping routines will keep you in control. In addition, there are a number of easy steps you can take to make each room in your home more accommodating to guests. We'll consider these two ideas next.

1 Establish regular housekeeping routines

One reason many people never invite others over—or even hide behind their curtains if the doorbell rings—is that their home always seems to be messy. They may spend an entire morning cleaning, only to despair a few days later when they notice new piles of paper stacked up on counters and the toy box's contents all over the living room floor.

My mother taught me to clear up messes as soon as I see them. If I spend just a few minutes throughout each day on a few designated house-hold routines, I find my day goes smoother and I am better prepared for anything—even surprise company. (I often get a lot done while on the phone.) My mother also taught me to have a routine for each week so everything is cleaned on a regular basis. I rarely get it all done but it helps to have a system to refer to. Oh, and it prevents a great deal of embarrassment, as well. Here's what I do:

Daily Routines

Morning
- Make bed or shut the door
- Clear and wipe dining table and countertops

- Clean up kitchen; empty and/or fill the dishwasher
- Wipe down bathroom counter with a towel that is going in the wash anyway
- Prepare God's workman (that's me) so I won't be ashamed. (In other words, I shower, put on makeup, and dress first thing in the morning.)

Late afternoon
- Tidy up the family room
- "Wash up as I mess up" while fixing dinner

After dinner
- Clear and wipe down dinner table
- Wash dishes and clean up kitchen

Before going to bed
- Oversee as the kids pick up their toys, books, etc.
- Tidy up family and living rooms

- Stash dishes from evening snacks and drinks in dishwasher; run dishwasher if it is full
- Recycle newspapers
- Locate the phone and put it back in the recharger

If the bedtime routine isn't done at night, I try to add it to the morning agenda.

Weekly Routines
- Dust furniture and knickknacks
- Sweep or vacuum floors
- Clean any obvious spots on floors
- Clean bathrooms

In kitchen
- Scrub sinks
- Clean under and behind things stored on countertops
- Get the stovetop back to its original color

- Wipe off obvious spots from the front of appliances and cupboards
- Sweep floor and mop up obvious spots

At this point you may think that I am very organized and probably have a detailed schedule for all the other housekeeping chores. I will tell you honestly that I do not. I am not that disciplined. I do all those other tasks as infrequently as I can. However, there are four things that motivate me to eventually do all that dirty work:

- It gets so bad that I can no longer stand it.
- Company is coming—either for a formal dinner party or an overnight visit.
- I am redecorating a room so I deep-clean it as it is put back together.
- My kids need something constructive to do.

Also remember that your chore lists will differ from mine because your family is not the Janssen Five who live on Nevermind Lane (yes, we really do!). The point is to develop your own daily systems so that the public areas never get so bad that you want to tack crime scene tape across your front door. It is easier to continually attack minor clutter than to once-in-a-blue-moon tackle gigantic intimidating messes.

I'll say it again, however: Do not let a messy or dirty home be your excuse for living the life of

Reality Check

As I began regularly sticking to my daily, and weekly, chores, I picked up some lessons in efficiency. I call them "Jo Ann's Fewer-Means-Less Principles of Housekeeping":

- The fewer pillows, throws, magazines, and knickknacks I keep around, the less I have to keep tidy.
- Fewer square feet of house mean less cleaning time.
- Fewer fabric furnishings like curtains, drapes, and tablecloths mean less work to keep them clean. It is easier to dust a dresser top than to shake out and occasionally wash and iron a dresser scarf or cloth.

a hermit. Remember that hospitality is not about impressing the people God puts in your life, but about blessing! (That is one reason why another part of my morning routine is spending some quiet time with God. I want my eyes to be open and my heart ready when he presents me with an opportunity to invite someone into my home.)

2 Don't try to go it alone!

Making your home guest-friendly and establishing housekeeping routines will make extending hospitality easier. Remember, however, that it might not be best to try to do everything yourself.

If you have the budget, some things can be hired out:

- Housecleaning
- Window washing
- Yard work
- Carpet cleaning

- Catering
- Shopping
- Party planning

I am too budget-conscious to spend money on things I can do myself or get my family to do. With a little training, my family can provide the following services to make my life easier while preparing for guests:

- Housecleaning
- Window washing
- Yard work
- Car washing
- Cleaning off deck and furniture
- Rearranging furniture
- Clearing out bathrooms for guests' use
- Making up beds
- Laundry
- Sweeping front sidewalk and stoop
- Cutting and arranging flowers
- Cleaning light fixtures

- Dusting high places and blinds
- Baby-proofing the house
- Baking cookies
- Cooking

If you work it right you may be able to lounge around with a clipboard and "supervise"! Also, don't forget that many family and friends are eager to help out when at your home. They can assist you and make other guests feel welcome by:

- Greeting guests
- Taking coats
- Keeping drinks and ice bucket filled
- Serving food
- Changing hand towels, checking toilet paper supply
- Taking photos
- Entertaining children
- Cleaning up

3 Survey each room

Why not take an inventory of your rooms now to see whether you can easily take any steps to make them more accommodating for guests who arrive at anytime? The ideas I offer below will make your home more inviting to your family as well.

The living room or family room

I believe in actually *using* the fancy living room. I know some people who have never allowed anyone into their formal living room. No occasion or person has yet been important enough. If you've spent time and effort on creating a formal living room, make your guests feel like VIPs by entertaining them there! If you do not have a formal living room, use whatever room you have, including your family room, den, or parlor. Any of these rooms can be arranged to put your guests at ease and encourage conversation.

4 Arrange comfortable, sturdy seating in conversational groups. Don't separate any two seats by more than eight or nine feet.

5 Make sure seating is arranged so that no one has to crane his or her neck around an obstacle to keep eye contact with others in the room.

6 Provide a handy surface for drinks and snacks for every seated person. Have coasters to protect delicate surfaces from water stains.

7 Have extra seats that can be brought in from other rooms. They do not have to match.

8 Know your crowd—sometimes floor pillows work even better than chairs!

9 Keep cords, decorative objects, toys, and other items out of the traffic areas to prevent injuries to people and things.

10 Stash some small toys and games appropriate for various ages to entertain the visitor who comes with kids.

The kitchen

The kitchen, of course, will be where you go to whip up coffee or other refreshments for your guests. By keeping your kitchen stocked with some basic items, you never have to divert your attention from your guests as you wonder what you could possibly offer them.

11 I keep our coffee mugs, coffee, teas, cream, and sugar all together near the stove to make it easy to offer and prepare a hot drink when someone stops by.

12 Store some sweets in the freezer and keep boxes of snack foods like crackers in your pantry.

13 Frozen dinners—homemade or not—also store well in the freezer.

14 Remember that with just eggs, milk, cheese, bread, and a small amount of fruit and vegetables you have everything you need for a complete meal—omelet, fruit, and toast any time of the day or night.

15 A Crock-Pot helps you work ahead and keeps things warm during a long dinner. When you are not sure exactly when company will arrive or when you have a busy day planned, consider planning a meal that you can prepare in your Crock-Pot.

16 Our cupboards hold more dinner plates and flatware than our family could ever dirty in a day. They come in handy when serving a crowd though. Real dishes, glasses, and flatware are so much sturdier than disposable. They are also cheaper in the long run and don't fill up landfills.

17 Keep a few baby items, like spoons, bib, and sipper cups, on hand.

18 Whatever you have to eat is there by God's provision—share generously. Christ praised the one who offers a glass of water in his name. Anyone can do that.

The dining room

Few of us ever will have the ideal dining room, but do not let inadequate tables and chairs stop you from extending invitations. Whatever you possess is sufficient for whatever God calls you to do right now. Soon after our marriage our first dinner guests lounged on the gold shag carpeting around a borrowed coffee table eating spaghetti on blue-light-special dishes! Here are some tips for making the most of your dining room.

19 For ideal dining, each guest should have twenty-four inches of table space.

20 To pull out a chair and sit at a table most comfortably, you need a minimum of forty-eight inches between the edge of the dining table and the closest obstacle, such as a wall or china cabinet.

21 The dining chair seat should be at about twelve inches from the lowest edge of the dining table.

22 Outdoor tables, card tables, and game tables (with their accompanying chairs) typically are about three inches shorter than dining room tables and chairs, which make mixing them up a bit tricky. Short chairs at a taller table make the diners feel like they are scooping their foods directly from the plate straight into their mouths since they are at about the same height. Taller chairs at short tables lead to bumped and bruised knees.

23 Do you need a new table quick? A flat door removed from its hinges (not from the bathroom door, please!) and placed across two sawhorses creates a large dining table.

24 Another idea: A round piece of plywood over a card table or similar square table enables you to seat more people. Just cover it with something pretty.

25 To assist with setting up, serving, and cleanup, use large trays and rolling carts, if they're available. Carts are also useful as an extra serving surface during a buffet, as are folding tables.

26 I prefer cloth napkins to paper ones. Cloth napkins stay on laps better, do not blow away, and are just plain easier to use. They make a guest feel more important. Plus, they are cheaper than paper in the long run.

27 Tablecloths can hide a lot of ugly scratches and stains. Sheets, blankets, clean tarps, lengths of fabric, and quilts can all serve as tablecloths.

The front porch

Even before they enter your home, visitors will sense whether they're welcome. Take a short stroll out your front door and look back toward your home. Is your home easy to find? Is it warm and inviting? If not, consider making the following changes.

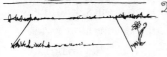

28 Use large house numbers that even people with myopic vision can easily see. (Am I the only nearsighted person who requires ten-inch numbers?)

29 If possible, illuminate your house number. You would be amazed at how many of your friends are getting a bit night blind. (Like me.)

30 Develop a parking plan you can use if you expect a crowd to need parking beyond your driveway and in front of your home. Perhaps neighbors would be willing to donate some parking spaces. Of course, you might offer to reciprocate when they have company. (It is a courtesy to inform them when you expect a crowd that may park in front of their home.)

31 Leave the front porch light on after dusk.

32 Sweep away dirt and cobwebs on your front porch.

33 Make a reproducible map to your home

Save time for yourself—and your guests— by creating a map to your home. I guarantee you'll use it again and again. I keep a file filled with copies of maps to our home. Some suggestions for your own map:

• Do not use the maps you can download from the Internet. They are extremely difficult to read and follow—and they are not always accurate.

- At the top of the map write your name, address, and phone number.
- Put a compass on the map showing directions.
- Neatly draw your map with major, well-known streets and intersections included for points of reference.
- Use a bold line to show roads to take to your home.
- Clearly label the streets people will use and the other streets around those to give points of reference. (If my guests pass Whileaway Drive, they know they have gone too far.)
- Sketch and label landmarks.
- Write in mileages. You actually may have to go out in your car and record the mileages that drivers will travel on each street on the way to your house.

- Somewhere on the page write out directions, using both "left and right" and "north, south, east, and west" directions. Include the landmarks (i.e. "First left after large white obelisk"), as well as a brief description of your home (i.e. "White marble, Federal-style two-story home with rose garden in front and guards at the gate").

- Ask someone to read your instructions to make sure they are very clear. Be aware that when landmarks change or you paint your house a new color you will have to edit the instructions.
- Put an X on the spot that represents your location with the house number next to it.

Once your home is ready, what's the next step? Welcoming guests, of course! In the next chapter, we'll look at how to create guest lists and welcome invited visitors to your home.

"Oh, Marilla, I've had a most fascinating time. I feel that I have not lived in vain and I shall always feel like that even if I should never be invited to tea at a manse again. When I got there Mrs. Allan met me at the door. She was dressed in the sweetest dress of pale-pink organdy, with dozens of frills and elbow sleeves, and she looked just like a seraph."

—ANNE SHIRLEY IN *ANNE OF GREEN GABLES* BY L. M. MONTGOMERY

Chapter 3
Be Our Guest

Weeks before the dinner party at Jim and Carol's, Al and I knew we were in for a special evening. They are outgoing people who share many of our interests. And Jim's hobby, we knew, was gourmet cooking.

Carol had checked on our availability and told us of her plans and who else she was inviting, so we anticipated not only fine food but also an evening filled with lively conversation. We were not disappointed.

The evening finally arrived. When our elegant hostess opened the door to greet us, our noses told us good things were cooking. She smiled and told us she was so happy we could make it. We followed Carol and the aromas to the kitchen where Jim was doing several things simultaneously. On the way I stopped to admire the dining room table. The dazzling setting included clear blue glass dishes and white plates, polished silver, starched white linens, and sparkling crystal.

Carol offered us beverages as Jim kept

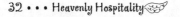

up a running commentary on his work. I asked if I could help and he put me to work stirring the whiskey sauce for the bread pudding. For a minute I felt like a real chef. It was a fleeting feeling, for soon all the guests had arrived. Dinner was served without delay.

Carol and Jim had spent considerable thought, time, and expense on the dinner's preparation. Every course was cooked to the kind of perfection that comes from years of practice. While savoring every bite, we laughed, lamented, and learned a lot about one another. Carol and Jim had thoughtfully considered the guest list, combining people from different life stages who had some things in common.

By the time anyone thought to check the time, we discovered it was much later than we expected. Grudgingly, we all did the mature thing and called it a night. On the way home Al and I remarked on how comfortable and welcome we had felt at Jim and Carol's. What can we learn from them? Let's begin by considering how to invite the right mix of people.

MAKING THE GUEST LIST

Consider three things when drawing up your guest list: 1) why you are having the event, 2) how many people you can accommodate, and 3) whom you wish to invite.

34 Determine the event's purpose first

What are some good reasons to host a party? They include:

- To introduce someone new to town
- To entertain a visiting VIP such as a missionary
- To get to know someone better

- To honor someone
- To bring people, such as neighbors on your street or acquaintances at church, together
- Evangelism
- To celebrate someone's birthday, anniversary, or other happy life event
- To develop new friendships
- Just for the fun of it

35 Estimate how many you can accommodate

Your home may not be as big as your heart, so be sure to consider how many you can comfortably fit. For my surprise fiftieth birthday tea party, my husband did not think that through. Our dining area can accommodate twelve people—maybe fourteen in a pinch. Twenty-four girlfriends attended. Thankfully, it was a typical warm, sunny day in May, so Al expanded the party to the back deck, which is adjacent to the dining room. Using some of my pretty table linens, china, and silverware, the deck was transformed into an elegant tea room. But what if the weather had not cooperated?

When determining how many people you can accommodate, keep the following in mind:

- You can squeeze a lot of people into a family room or living room if you are planning a meeting or shower that will last only a few hours. If the room opens to an adjacent kitchen or dining room, you may be able to fit even more. Don't forget: some people are comfortable seated on the floor. Older people generally like comfortable chairs. Know your crowd.
- You can probably invite a lot of people to parties at which people will spend most of the time standing up, such as an open house. This kind of party works well when you want to honor someone. One of my writing colleagues hosts an open house each time

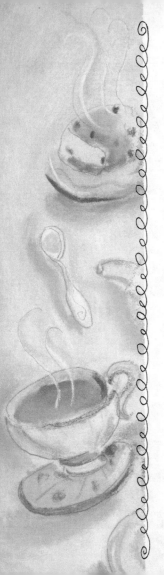

one of her books comes out. Graduates, visiting VIPs, couples celebrating a milestone anniversary, and newlyweds can all be recognized at an open house.

- At holiday dinners, consider whether it would be possible to squeeze more table space into one room. We put a small drop-leaf table end-to-end with our dining room table to fit everyone.
- Can you take the party outside? Do not limit yourself to the table and four chairs on the cement slab outside your back door. Expand to the lawn with picnic blankets or card tables.
- How many young children can you realistically handle? They need space. They need entertaining. They need to go to bed at a reasonable hour. They make messes, touch everything, knock things over, go where they are not supposed to go, and so on. As much as you may love them, do not let

yourself in for more than you can handle. Know your home, know your personal endurance level, and be realistic.

These events will require you to use

Reality Check

Be careful about using a separate kids' table at holiday dinners. How old does someone have to be before they graduate to the adult table?

Twenty-some years ago my in-laws had Al and me and his sister, Frances, to their home for Thanksgiving dinner. We "kids" were all in our late twenties and well into our chosen career. However, when it was time to eat, we three youngsters were seated at a flimsy card table butted up against the dining room table where Mama and Papa Janssen sat. Since we were sitting on chairs that went with the dining room table, our knees kept knocking against the card table. Though there was plenty of room at the dining room table, we were the "kids" and so we sat at the kids' table. Since that one strange experience, Al and I have always hosted family holiday dinners. While Al's parents are now gone and we miss them at our holiday dinners, we never did find out when we would have been old enough to sit at the dining room table!

all your social skills to make everyone feel special.

36 Decide whom to invite

Finally it's time to decide whom to invite. Creating the right mix of people—think of it as social engineering—can be the recipe for a successful get-together. If you are inviting people who do not know one another, it is important to consider how well they might get along together. You might ask yourself the following:

- Will your guests share a common interest? Perhaps they all sing in the choir, play the same sport, love the Broncos, enjoy the same hobby, have the same kind of job, or come from the same tiny town in the Midwest.
- Make sure that you invite a few talented conversationalists, or it will be a quiet and painful time for everyone.
- Consider strong personal views. It may

not be wise to invite the owner of the corner liquor store to the same dinner party as the president of the local chapter of MADD.

- If you are introducing someone new to town, make sure everyone knows that is the purpose of the event so the newcomer will be the center of attention and not feel left out of conversations between old friends. I have a painful memory as a newcomer at a ladies luncheon that was set up to introduce me to some women whose husbands would be working with mine at his new job. During the meal the other three ladies thoughtlessly made arrangements for other get-togethers that excluded me. I felt so left out.
- Will all the guests enjoy

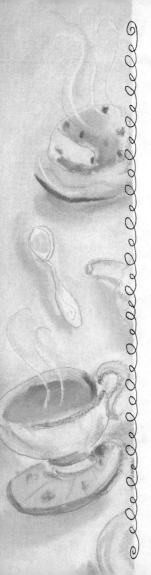

what you have planned? I wouldn't invite someone apathetic about football to a Super Bowl party. Likewise, most guys would not enjoy a chick-flick party.

- Will you be including children? If so, they may need a separate program and menu. What if you want to invite Alice and her well-behaved kids but not Emily with her less disciplined brood? The only way out is to have no children at all. Find a way to tactfully include that information in the invitation.

37 Making your guests feel welcome

Our friends Jim and Carol not only thought through the logistics of their dinner party, they ensured that everyone who attended felt like a valued guest. It began with the invitation and continued with their thoughtful gestures through-out the party. Here's how you can make your guests feel welcome too:

- Make the invitation warm and inviting. Homemade invitations convey a lot of care. The prepackaged variety can be warmed up with a handwritten note saying you hope they can make it. The verbal invitation can be the most welcoming because you can express your anticipation with your own words and tone.
- To give the outside of your home a welcoming feeling, see my ideas for the front porch on page 28 of chapter 2.
- Greet small crowds at the door as they arrive. When Al and I arrived at Bob and Trudy's house for dinner recently, they came out to the front porch when they saw us drive up. They greeted us with hugs and smiles. New friends instantly felt like old friends. Not everyone is comfortable receiving a hug, but by showing your pleasure at seeing your guests you can convey the same feeling. This is one time when warm is cool.

- The larger the crowd, the trickier it is to make guests feel welcome. Your challenge is to have a few words with guests individually to let them know you are glad to see them in your home. There is an exception to this rule. When my sister, Sue, hosted a class reunion in her spacious home, she did not feel compelled to try to greet, much less talk to, each guest. When the crowd is coming to your home because it is the location of a big event—rather than at your personal invitation—you are not obligated to speak to each one.

- Remember to do as much as you can as far ahead as you can. Get yourself and your home ready early so final food preparations are all you need to do at the last minute. Guests can keep you company in the kitchen as you finish. However, they will not be amused if you keep them waiting in the living room while you apply cosmetics. Last week a friend of mine was due for lunch at my home at noon. She arrived fifteen minutes early. Fortunately, I had followed my own advice and was ready for her.

- No matter how frenzied you feel before guests arrive, as soon as you hear the doorbell ring, take a deep breath, smile, and calm yourself before opening the door.

- Once the party begins, you need to ensure that no one feels left out. Look around. Does everyone have someone to talk with? If not, do some social engineering. Go to the lonely individual or couple and say that you would like them to meet the so-and-so's (whom you know to be friendly). Chat with the newly formed small group until the conversation can continue without you.

- When introducing strangers, mention something they have in common or something of interest to both parties.

- Keep an eye and ear out not only for the

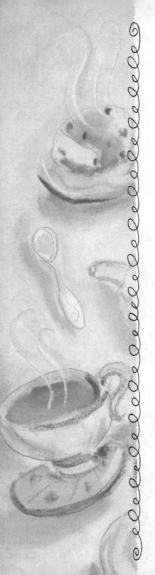

lonely but for the obnoxious. As the host, you must help keep overbearing personalities under control, tactfully mend hurt feelings, and monitor the ambiance of your party.

Sometimes you'll need to help the conversation take a U-turn. Be aware of gossip, backstabbing, complaining, lecturing, or other un-Christian talk. Cheerfully but firmly change the subject. The tried-and-true way is to say "Nice weather we're having, isn't it?" Most people will take the hint.

• The difference between calm, welcoming Jim and Carol and a frazzled couple like Paul and Elly often comes down to their planning. Use my lists in the appendix to get organized and stay in control.

• How do you keep that welcoming feeling when your company won't leave? Last Saturday night our host looked at his watch at about 10 P.M. and cheerfully said, "Oh, my! Look at the time. We all need to get to bed so we can get to church on time tomorrow morning." Since the host was a church music director, everyone quickly got the message. While honesty is often the best policy, be sure to let your guests know that you regret how quickly the time has gone. Then get up, get your guests' coats, and move toward the front door. Barely stifle your yawn but keep smiling.

• The next time you see your guests, mention how much you enjoyed their company. Find reasons to get together again.

Now that you have mastered the fine art of making your planned guests feel welcome, it is time to think about extending those same techniques to the unexpected guests.

"I am just about to take tea; pray come and have some with me."

—Bilbo Baggins to strangers who have rung his front doorbell. From *The Hobbit* by J. R. R. Tolkien

Chapter 4
Welcoming Unexpected Guests

During a very stressful time in her life, my friend Karen took long walks. One Saturday morning she realized she was on my street and noticed that my front door was open. She bravely knocked, hoping I was home. I was.

My cooking and cleaning for that evening's dinner party seemed unimportant in the face of her pain. I listened for a couple of hours as we drank ice water and she vented her hurt and anger. That is what friends are for. And somehow all the preparation for the meal that night got done.

As a Christian I find it helpful to regard every human encounter as a God-ordained opportunity to bless. Usually I am the one who ends up feeling encouraged. Welcoming people into our homes and schedules allows that to happen—even when we are not expecting them!

38 The Fifteen-Minute Tea Party

Just because a friend drops by unexpectedly does not mean making her feel special must cause you stress. When a girlfriend stops by

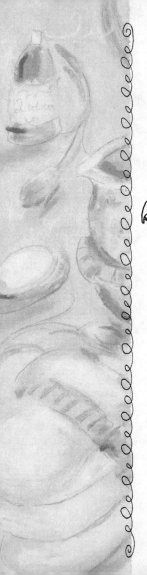

and has more than fifteen minutes, I treat her to my Fifteen-Minute Tea Party. I call it the Fifteen-Minute Tea Party because that is approximately how much time it takes to concoct, not how long it lasts! Also, it is easy enough that I can invite my friend to keep me company— or even help me—while I produce an elegant tea party. Here's how it is done:

Heat oven to 450°.

Fill teakettle or pot with water and put it on stove on high heat.

Gather the following ingredients to quickly whip up these great-tasting scones. (The recipe can easily be doubled if you have more than four people sitting down to tea.)

1 ¼ cup all-purpose flour*
1 ½ teaspoons baking powder
½ teaspoon salt
2 teaspoons sugar
2 tablespoons butter or margarine
1 egg
¼ cup milk
sugar
¼ cup blueberries, raisins, Craisins, or chocolate chips (optional)

Mix dry ingredients in mixing bowl.

Use a pastry cutter to cut in the butter or margarine until it looks mealy.

In a small bowl beat together the egg and milk (or omit the egg and use a little more milk). Mix it into the flour mixture. If necessary, add more milk until dough holds together. Add berries or chocolate chips if desired.

*At higher altitudes, decrease flour to 1 cup. Add milk or flour as needed.

Form the dough into a ball and knead it a dozen times.

Apply nonstick cooking spray to a cookie sheet; place the ball of dough in the center of it.

Pat the dough into a circle about 6 inches wide and ¾ inch deep. Use a knife to cut it into 4–6 wedges. Sprinkle the tops with sugar.

Place it in the oven for 8–10 minutes. The scones are done when they look golden brown on top.

Meanwhile have your friend rinse out your favorite teapot with hot water and put tea bags in it. When the water boils fill the teapot.

While the tea is steeping and the scones are baking, set the table with your favorite tea cups and small plates (they do not have to match); spoons, forks, knives, and napkins; cream and sugar; butter; jam or jelly in a bowl.

Set aside a serving plate for the scones. Line it with a paper doily if you have one handy.

If all works well, the scones, tea, and table setting should be completed at about the same time. If not, enjoy the company and laugh about how it did not work out as planned!

39 Oh, look! It's lunchtime

Occasionally you may decide on the spur of the moment to invite a guest to stay for lunch. Perhaps a friend arrives unannounced at 11:30 A.M. (making you wonder whether she came expecting a brief chat or was planning to get a free lunch). Or maybe she comes earlier in the morning. After you talk awhile, you discover that time has flown by so fast that it is lunchtime, but you want to continue your conversation. In either case, what do you do? Invite your visitor to stay for lunch, of course. Now, what do you serve?

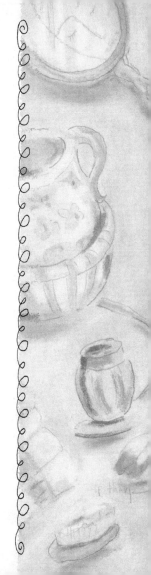

Since this is an unexpected event, your guests probably will have low expectations. But you want to make it as gracious as possible.

You probably have the makings of a decent lunch lurking in your fridge. For a simple menu, here's what I do:

Find some leftover meat or a small can of tuna. Chopped meat is the basis of "Jo Ann's Secret Salad for Sandwiches."

Finely chop up a tablespoon or so of onion.

Dice a tablespoon or so of veggies and/ or fresh herbs, such as celery, green peppers, cilantro, parsley, cucumber, garlic, or tomato.

Combine ingredients; mix them together with a dollop of mayonnaise. (Add a pinch of curry if chicken or turkey is your base.)

Create an open- or closed-faced sand- wich using sandwich bread, English muffins, biscuits, bagels, focaccia bread, hamburger buns, French bread, or dinner rolls.

Put the sandwich on a plate. (I use my pretty blue willow plates to make my humble fare look more impressive.) Slice it down the middle then place the halves on either side of the plate.

Cut up some fresh veggies or fruit into uniform pieces and lay them artistically between the sandwich halves. If all you have is canned fruit, serve it in small bowls.

Set the table with your best dishes and cloth napkins to dress up the spread.

Beverages need not be fancy. Most people just drink water at meals anyway. Offer what you have. If you have a lemon, place a wedge in the iced water.

Dessert is not required but if you have any sweets around the house, serve them attractively. Presentation is everything.

Other fast lunch alternatives include canned soup, a salad of fresh veggies and chopped meats, an omelet, leftovers, delivered pizza, or fast food.

40 Spruce up your service

Using elegant dinnerware can transform a casual visit into something special. The fancy kitchenware that you may have accumulated over the years might make any occasion more genteel but they are not essential for a meaningful meal.

Over the years I've collected quite a few lovely serving pieces. Some are family heirlooms. Others were gifts from friends who know my affinity for tea-party paraphernalia. I've also picked up some items at yard sales and grocery store promotions. More than likely you have some special items too. All of the following can make the Fifteen-Minute Tea Party—or luncheon—special.

- China tea pot, cups, plates, and bowls
- Silverware and serving pieces (Mine are a happy unmatched mix of family heirlooms and thrift store finds.)
- Pretty cloth napkins and tablecloths
- Paper doilies (available at Wal-Mart)
- Floral centerpieces (I lucked out here: My best friend is a floral designer.)

I also keep sugar cubes and sugar-cube tongs (a family heirloom) in a covered china sugar bowl. New ones can usually be found in shops that sell all the fine accoutrements involved with elegant tea parties. They make welcome, inexpensive gifts. Boxes of sugar cubes are usually stocked near the boxes and bags of various kinds of sugars in the baking supply aisle at your local grocery store.

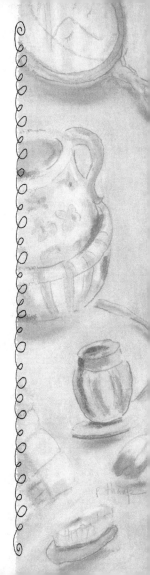

⟨⟨⟨⟨⟨⟨ Reality Check ⟨⟨⟨⟨⟨⟨⟨

I've learned that unexpected guests do not generally stop by because they

- Sadistically want to add to the pain of an already stressful situation
- Intend to give you some unwelcome advice or add to your guilt
- Wish to critique your décor or give your home the white-glove treatment
- Expect to receive a gourmet snack or meal
- Are irrepressibly nosy
- Want to see for themselves if your new house/baby/ decorating/car/haircut/plastic surgery is really as awful as they heard it is

Instead I've come to realize that they usually show up because they

- Are lonely, hurting, or bored
- Need someone to talk to
- Know you are hurting and want to share the burden
- Are just passing through town and realize their schedule allows time for a visit
- Have some wonderful news they feel they must share with someone before they burst

- See your light is on and realize they haven't talked to you in ages
- Heard about your new house/baby/decorating/car/ haircut/plastic surgery and want to share your joy

So think the best and savor the surprise!

THE UNEXPECTED DINNER GUESTS

At times you may need to scramble to prepare a dinner for unexpected dinner guests. That isn't uncommon in our household.

One summer afternoon I cleaned out our refrigerator to clear it before some houseguests arrived that evening. Using the contents of the little containers of leftovers I found there, I made my family's dinner.

Just as we Janssen Five were about to sit down to our individually assembled salads made of leftover meats and veggies and a basket full of bits and pieces of leftover breads, the doorbell rang. Our three houseguests had arrived two hours early without warning. After the squeals of surprise and happy hugs we joyfully set more places at the table. Then it was time to pray for a loaves-and-fishes type of miracle.

I sent the kids to our vegetable garden to harvest as many veggies as they could. After quickly washing and cutting them up, I deftly rearranged the meats and other goodies from the five salads I had previously assembled and was able to create three more salads. We had enough bread to go around (thank you, Lord!) and the homemade cookies were well received. We enjoyed a wonderful time with our dear old friends.

On other occasions my big-hearted husband has called in the late afternoon asking me if he could invite a guy from Somewhereville to our house for dinner. The answer is always yes.

Last minute guests do not expect a five-course gourmet meal. They are usually just thrilled to be invited for dinner in the first place. Neither do they expect an immaculate house. I generally ask my daughter to make sure the guest bathroom is decent. My boys quickly pick up stray items in the public areas.

QUICK DINNER EXPANSION TRICKS

Most evenings I try to cook enough dinner to have leftovers. For that reason unexpected guests are generally not a problem. However, at times I've had to quickly figure out how to expand dinner so there will be enough for guests. This has occurred often enough for me to offer the following tips.

41 For a nonpasta dinner

The quickest addition is potatoes, which really fill people up. If I hastily pare and cut any kind of potato into small-sized cubes they cook in very little time. After I mash the cooked potatoes I put them in a casserole dish and top them with grated cheese and melt it in the oven. If I have sour cream or green onions, I add them to the mashed potatoes.

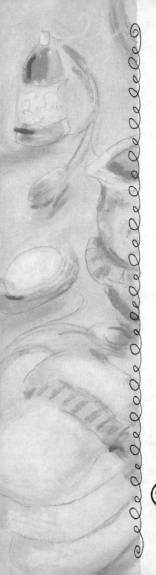

42 For a pasta dinner

Cook more pasta than originally planned. It is all right to mix up pastas. I have combined fettuccine and spaghetti; broken up spaghetti into small pieces and added it to elbow macaroni; served spaghetti sauce over almost every kind of pasta; and probably breached every noodle etiquette in existence!

43 For a soup or stew dinner

To boost the volume of a stew or soup (or even a spaghetti sauce), add one or more of the following:

- A can of tomato sauce
- A can of vegetables or beans
- Diced potatoes
- Diced onions
- Almost any diced or pureed vegetable
- Quick-cooking rice
- Small pastas such as elbow macaroni and small shell macaronis. Break up long, skinny pastas like linguini, spaghetti, or fettuccine into small pieces.
- A can of compatible soup
- A handful of whole grains like oats or barley that will cook in the available time

44 For any meal

Add bread

- Ask your spouse to pick up a loaf of Italian or French bread on the way home.
- Whip up some biscuits. Bisquick is, uh, quick, or use my scone recipe without the sugar. (You will probably have to double it.)
- Toast some slices of sandwich bread, then spread butter, Parmesan cheese, and garlic salt on them.

Add another side dish

- Cook up another vegetable.
- Add a tossed green salad.

• Learn the fine art of making a Jell-O salad set really fast using ice cubes.
• Heat up some leftovers.

45 Perfect your presentation

Transform your humble offerings into gourmet fare by practicing attractive presentation techniques. To dress up the food:

• Serve all foods in attractive containers.
• Arrange cuts of meat neatly on a platter.
• Garnish entrees with grated cheese, croutons, parsley, veggie curls, or a chopped veggie sprinkled artfully over or around them.
• For pasta-and-sauce dinners, pile the pasta on a large platter or in a large bowl and pour the sauce on top. Grate some cheese over the middle of the sauce.
• Serve butter on a butter dish with a butter serving knife. (Make sure your kids know the butter knife is solely for the purpose of transporting the butter from the butter dish to their personal plate, and not for spreading.)
• Beautify dessert with a swirl of ice-cream topping.
• Set the table with your best linens and plates or china and stemware.
• Use bread plates with your table setting. Saucers work well for bread. They go above the fork of each person's setting.
• Turn down the lights and burn candles.

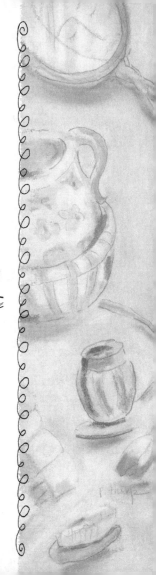

When I forget about myself for a few hours and concentrate on the person God has unexpectedly brought into my home, I find myself having a delightful time. Our family fondly recalls numerous occasions when we have allowed God to bring people into our home and forgotten about our imperfect

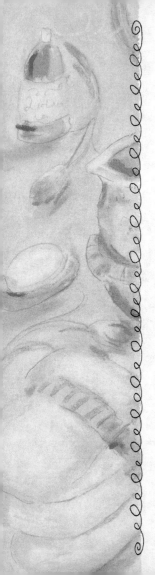

housekeeping, humble foods, and tattered furniture. I guess it boils down to a choice. Will
I be selfish and prideful, worried about the
impressions I am making? Or will I be selfless
and think of others? Do I aim to impress
or bless?

Mix a pancake, stir a pancake, pop it in the pan; fry the pancake, toss the pancake—catch it if you can.

—Christina Georgina Rossetti,
New Treasury of Children's Poetry

Chapter 5
Simple Starters

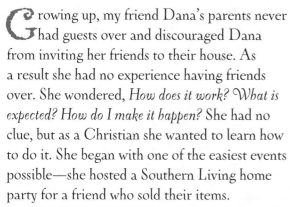rowing up, my friend Dana's parents never had guests over and discouraged Dana from inviting her friends to their house. As a result she had no experience having friends over. She wondered, *How does it work? What is expected? How do I make it happen?* She had no clue, but as a Christian she wanted to learn how to do it. She began with one of the easiest events possible—she hosted a Southern Living home party for a friend who sold their items.

The Southern Living representative helped her with a timeline of when to do what to make it happen. The invitations, provided by the company, were sent on schedule. The day before the party Dana cleaned her living room, powder room, and kitchen, and she made cookies. The day of the party she did a last-minute pickup around the house. An hour before the party was to begin the representative came to set up while Dana brewed coffee and tea. On her kitchen table she arranged her mismatched coffee mugs, cream and sugar, spoons, paper napkins, and a plate of cookies.

When the doorbell rang Dana was ready,

relaxed, and raring to party! When you get a bunch of friendly women together success is guaranteed. The ladies laughed and talked and purchased pretty things. The last guest left an hour past the expected end of the party because Dana and her friend had been talking and lost track of the time. The party was not only a success, but it gave Dana the experience and confidence she needed to try again.

As you begin to practice hospitality you too may want to begin with small gatherings that do not require much work. While Dana carefully planned her party, many occasions for hospitality naturally present themselves in everyday life. Take advantage of them. Here are some of my suggestions on where to begin.

46 The coffee break

The most common and easiest form of hospitality is the one-on-one chat with a neighbor or friend. The kitchen table or living room that is kid- and clutter-free is a cozy, comfortable place to sit and sip. My friend Elly should have started small with this sort of occasion. How do you prepare for it?

First, make sure you have the ingredients for whatever beverage you want to serve. Cold drinks can be prepared ahead. Do a quick once-over of any room your neighbor might see. Call that neighbor you have been meaning to connect with and say something like, "I was just about to sit down with a cup of coffee [or a glass of iced tea or whatever] and thought how nice it would be if you could join me. Could you come over in about fifteen minutes? I would really like it if you could!"

After she says she would be delighted to come over, start the hot beverage. Pull two everyday mugs or tea cups out of the cupboard, make sure there is sugar in the sugar bowl, and fill the creamer with milk. If you decide to serve some goodies, place them on a plate. With finger foods, you will just need napkins. With fancier desserts such as cake, you will need dessert plates, forks, and napkins. You may want to follow my instructions for the Fifteen-Minute Tea Party found on page 39. Decide where you will sit.

When the doorbell rings, welcome your guest with a smile and invite her into the kitchen to get the beverages. Invite her to make herself comfortable. Treat her as if she is the most important person in the world. Act as if there is nothing you would rather do than get to know her. Let the answering machine catch your phone calls. If the conversation is lagging, ask leading questions, such as "Where are you from?" "What brought you to our little town?" "Tell me about your family," "What are your hobbies?" Look for common interests. It could be the beginning of a beautiful friendship.

47 Kids for lunch

Your kids and their friends are playing together and getting along so well. You are actually able to get some things done around the house as the children entertain each other. It would be a shame to send the friends home for lunch and ruin the spell. Phone the mothers and see if they can stay for lunch. The other moms will probably acquiesce because they are finally getting some stuff done around their house as well!

You know what your offspring like to eat, but be sure to ask their friends. Peanut butter and jelly sandwiches (assuming they have no allergies to peanuts) are usually a safe bet.

Don't be surprised if the kids don't eat much. Kids generally do not eat as much away from home as they would at home. They are excited. They are eager to get back to their

game. The food is different. You cut the fruit into bigger pieces than they are accustomed to. You have grape jelly instead of the strawberry jam they use at home.

Other lunch possibilities include macaroni and cheese made from a boxed mix, cheese pizza, or soup. Plain pasta of any kind served with a bit of butter is acceptable to most picky eaters. My own children like it with Parmesan cheese that they personally sprinkle on top.

Serve small portions simply. Fill glasses only half full. Have plenty of napkins handy. Do not be too strict about them eating all their carrot sticks before indulging in a brownie. Be calmly firm in reminding your own children about their manners. This is a learning and training time, not only for you, but for your children.

48 Hosting meetings
(Bible studies, committee meetings, board meetings, Moms in Touch, rehearsals, group projects)

It seems life can go on only if we meet to discuss it regularly. One advantage to all these meetings is that they offer great opportunities for practicing some low-stress hospitality. What does it take to host a meeting? I've learned a lot from my good friend Ingrid.

Ingrid hosts a Chamber Singers rehearsal on Wednesday nights and a women's Bible study on Thursday mornings. She does her weekly housecleaning Wednesday mornings. This savvy friend says that a house cleaned once a week is easier to spruce up and keep clean than one that is neglected for several weeks at a time.

Just before everyone shows up for either event she makes a pot of coffee and heats up some water for the tea drinkers. Beverages are served on the kitchen counter next to the stove where the tea water stays hot and the coffeemaker is plugged in. She keeps her mugs, a container filled with a variety of teas, and her creamer and sugar set stored nearby. She places a few spoons next to the mugs. Her friends know where all this is kept and feel free to help set up if Ingrid is running behind schedule. Because Ingrid is not uptight, everyone feels welcome in her home. (She would be the first one to laugh if someone found a dead bug in a coffee mug.)

About fifteen minutes before everyone is expected, Ingrid opens her front door. The screen door offers a view of the entrance hall and the welcoming kitchen beyond. Everyone knows they are just to walk right in so Ingrid isn't constantly rushing to the front door.

Chairs are brought into her living room from all over the house. Some people prefer to sit on the floor. There is always room for one more!

Ingrid makes it appear easy to host meet-ings. That is because it is. Homes are more conducive to comfortable conversation than a cold meeting room in the church basement.

Most of us have the tools: seating, coffee mugs, teaspoons, something to serve cream and sugar in, a coffeemaker. If you haven't accumulated the above list of things, you probably have some drinking glasses stored in your kitchen cupboard and ice in your freezer. A glass of water is always an accept-able offering.

The next time your committee/panel/Bible study/board needs a place to meet, consider offering your home. You will be serving others and gaining more hands-on experience in hospitality.

49 Great friends for dinner at the last minute

The least intimidating dinner guests are the ones who have loved you for a long time and will continue to love you no matter what.

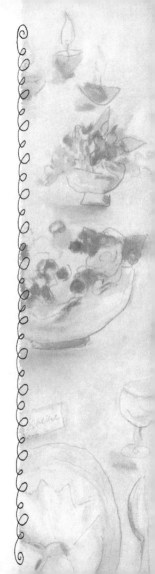

They are the perfect people on which to practice your hospitality skills.

Whether you extend the invitation a month or an hour ahead of time, your friends will come not to judge but to enjoy your company. Our friends, the Fords, are just such friends. We can call them Friday afternoon and suggest we get together for dinner and some card games. It doesn't matter to either of us who will host the evening. We talk over the logistics of our families' busy lives and decide on the best location.

The meal is usually a few pizzas from our local Papa Murphy's You-Bake 'N Save. Their pies are much cheaper than delivered pizza, and we get to enjoy the wonderful aromas of pizza baking. On the way home from picking them up, we stop at the grocery store for ice cream and toppings. If we have green salad and/or homemade cookies, those are served as well.

When we host the evening I feel no pressure to make sure the house is perfectly clean. Anna wipes down the bathroom and hides her cosmetics. I sweep the floor if the dust bunnies have become too noticeable, and I tidy up the kitchen.

The six Fords and Janssen Five squeeze around the dining room table and catch up on news, laugh, and have a great time. We still expect our children to practice their best manners. No one throws food. We politely ask to have things passed. The fact that the Fords and the Janssens are both concerned that their children grow up practicing good manners is one of the many things we have in common—and another advantage of our casual dinners.

50 One step further with good friends

Those same trusted friends can be the ones on whom you practice more formal dinners. Make the date a couple of weeks in advance and let them know what to expect. Your dear friend will probably want to contribute something to the meal. Let her.

Practice the menu on your family before serving it to guests. After you have assured yourself that it tastes great and is well within your level of abilities, put it on your list of things to serve company.

Although I am not a gourmet cook (my husband just agreed a little *too* heartily) I have collected a few recipes that my friends and family always rave about. Some I got from friends, some from cookbooks, and a couple I actually perfected myself. I encourage you to begin your own personal collection of such dishes.

To make the most of this experience, plan everything on paper. Write down when you will shop, clean house, and prepare foods. Make a detailed guide for completing the meal at the designated time. Then follow your plan!

If anything goes wrong your friends will still love you. I learned that the time I served pecan pie to our friends the Ostens. Before adding the filling, I had neglected to remove the wax paper that lined the frozen piecrust. We laughed as we scooped pie filling out of the crust with a spoon. We still laugh together over this memory.

51 Dessert after the show

You are meeting some friends to see a play or movie and decide it would be fun to discuss it afterward over pie and coffee. Unfortunately your town, like ours, rolls up its sidewalks at 10 P.M. This is the ideal opportunity to practice some easy hospitality.

The preparations will include a light house-cleaning, purchasing or making a dessert, and getting the coffeemaker ready. Our local price

club sells a cheesecake that is always a huge success if I do not have time to bake. I suggest serving *decaf* beverages. Try to set out the coffee cups, dessert plates, spoons and forks, napkins, and your cream and sugar set ahead of time.

Your living room will be the ideal setting, especially if you followed my advice in chapter 2 to arrange your seating into a conversation group and have table surfaces available for coffee cups and dessert plates.

Call your friends before the event to invite them over. When you get home after the show, turn on the coffeemaker and serve the dessert. It couldn't be easier!

52 Hosting the sports event party

Sporting events, which include the Super Bowl, World Series, NBA Finals, and World Cup, offer an activity of interest that is easy to plan a party around. When the next big event comes up and you decide you want to invite the gang to watch it with you, what do you have to do to make it happen?

After you issue the invitations, you will need to plan what you will serve, when you will clean the house, and what accommodations you will make for everyone to view the game or event.

A few general hints about preparing for this kind of party follow. After that, I offer some tips on preparing food and your home.

- Invite your guests to wear apparel with team logos and colors. Friendly rivalries will spice up the excitement!
- Put away good rugs and breakable knick-knacks.
- Provide coasters for drinks.
- Have plenty of paper napkins and sturdy paper plates on hand.

Food

Most work: Spend days preparing finger foods.

Less work: Purchase prepared platters at the grocery store or price club.

Least work: Make the party a potluck event.

Beverages

Most work: Prepare punch, iced tea, lemonade, hot cocoa, hot tea, and coffee.

Less work: Purchase a variety of cans of soda. Keep them chilled in a tub of ice.

Least work: Assign drinks to one of the party goers. Assign ice to another.

Housework

Most work: Clean every square inch of the house.

Less work: Clean just the TV room, kitchen, and bathroom.

Least work: Pick up the clutter in the TV room, kitchen, and bathroom. Nobody will notice anyway.

Seating

Most work: Make sure everyone will have a cushy seat with a place to put his or her own drinks and food nearby.

Less work: Throw some pillows on the floor. Add a couple of chairs.

Least work: What you see is what you get. You know where to find an extra chair if you need one.

During the party do not let yourself become a slave to your spouse and the guests. Make yourself comfortable and let your friends know that they can help themselves. It will be easier to relax if all the goodies, napkins, and plates are set up on a table in or near the TV room.

No matter how much or how little work you put into the preparations, you can be

assured of a great time when you invite great friends. Quantity of food and drink become more important than quality. Your friends will be having too much fun to judge your house-keeping.

SUNDAY DINNER

Many of the lessons I learned about hospitality as a child I learned at Sunday dinner. Every Saturday after our evening meal of hamburgers

ᘒᘒᘒᘒᘒᘒᘒ Reality Check ᗕᗕᗕᗕᗕᗕᗕ

My mom's traditional Sunday dinner and my humbler one have a few things in common:

• They can be prepared ahead of time.
• They are simple.
• They require no thought because the recipes are tried and true.
• The family helps as much as they are able.
• They provide an easy yet ideal opportunity to invite guests to dinner.

(menu planning is made easier if you serve the same thing every Saturday and Sunday), my mom would prepare the roast, pare the carrots, peel the potatoes, and slice some onions. She had baked a pie or cake earlier in the day. Before leaving for church the next morning she would brown the roast, then add the vege-tables and some liquid to the electric frying pan (the predecessor of the Crock-Pot). When we returned from church—often with dinner guests—our home would welcome us with the most heavenly aromas.

Dad liked to eat as soon as possible, because he was hungry after a morning of preaching and pastoring. Mom quickly tied an apron around her waist, transferred the hot food to platters, and covered them. While one of us kids set the table, she whisked up delicious brown gravy. Rolls, butter, pickles, jam, and salt and pepper went to the table. By the time all six Pulsiphers and guests had washed their hands, dinner was served. The roast beef dinner was a surefire success every time.

Dad knew he was free to invite guests for Sunday dinner because there was always plenty of good food that Mom was proud to serve. Our home was always cleaned on Saturday, so my parents didn't have to worry about that either.

As much as I treasure the memories of those dinners, my life is very different from my mother's. Sunday is my day off. Cooking is work for me and I refuse to do it on Sundays. But the Janssen Five still like to have people over for Sunday dinner after church.

Since I don't cook on Sundays, how do the Janssen Five pull off a company Sunday dinner? We have two ways. One type is planned; the other is used for guests we've invited on the spur of the moment.

53 The five-star Sunday brunch

If we have thought ahead and extended an invitation, we serve a brunch menu. We prepare it all on Saturday. The tried-and-true menu includes muffins, fruit salad, a bacon, egg, and cheese casserole (many cookbooks contain  recipes for breakfast casseroles), juice, coffee, and tea. Dessert is optional. My oven has a time-delay baking option that I use to have the casserole just about done when we walk in the door from church.

If there is time, we set the table before leaving for church. If not, my kids quickly do it when we get home. If the weather is gloriously gorgeous, as it often is in Colorado Springs, we eat outside on our covered deck. Guests *love* it out there! My husband has to yawn conspicuously to get rid of them.

54 The pancake house

Our spur-of-the-moment meal consists of our usual Sunday menus. We alternate between French toast with a fruit topping one week and pancakes the next. If company comes we add cheesy scrambled eggs. Besides habitually keeping grated cheese in the freezer and eggs in the refrigerator, we also have orange juice, tea, and coffee on hand. Dessert is not usually offered or needed.

It takes my sons just a few minutes to add leaves to our dining room table and gather more chairs. Everyone works together to make it happen. (Hunger is the great motivator.) One of the kids mixes up the orange juice; another fills the syrup pitcher; another fills a clean butter dish; and everyone helps carry things to the table. My husband does all the cooking. Remember, it is my day off!

As a wedding present twenty-six years ago we received a large nonstick griddle that cooks multiple pancakes or slices of French toast at once. Each batch is then transferred to a plate and kept in a warm oven until enough have been cooked to feed that day's crowd.

We upgrade our humble menus by using our best table linens and china. We even use them outside. Trays make it easier to set and clear the table.

After you have had a few fairly successful simple social events in your home you may be ready to branch out to the more complicated dinner party. The next chapter is just what you need.

"I suppose you will all stay to supper?" he said in his politest unpressing tones.

—Bilbo to Gandalf and other surprise visitors
in *The Hobbit* by J. R. R. Tolkien

Chapter 6
Dinner Parties

Soon after our wedding Al and I invited two friends, who happened to be professional athletes in town for the weekend, to dinner at our apartment. Since there were only four of us, we were able to squeeze around our little drop-leaf table in the kitchen. I had prepared my famous spaghetti dinner and Al was proudly serving it. As he pivoted from the stove to the table with a plateful of food, momentum took over. Al and the plate stopped but the entree kept on going! That slippery pasta flew ever so neatly from the plate to one guest's lap.

After a stunned group gasp, we all laughed and cleaned up the mess. And yet another wonderful memory was added to our rich lives!

A dinner party can be anything from a formal sit-down dinner to a backyard potluck buffet. I suggest starting out with more casual events with close friends (who will be very polite when you dump dinner on their lap) to gain confidence and expertise before inviting the boss over for standing rib roast. Use

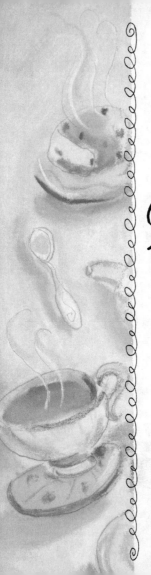

appendix A to help you plan all the details and have time to spare.

The right combination of people makes an enjoyable event for everyone, so I begin my planning with the guest list. Actually, Al and I have an ever-growing list of people we want to include in our dinner parties. (So many people, so little time!) See chapter 3 for suggestions on how to create a winning guest list.

Planning your menu

Through trial and error I have learned some things to make my menus easier to plan and execute.

55 Serve dishes you are comfortable preparing, or plan to practice making any new dishes to see whether you can prepare them successfully. New recipes also need to be taste-tested. (We failed to do that once. Our friend Ron was pretty frantic after he took the first bite of the spiciest chili ever made!)

56 When possible, find out if any of your guests have food allergies or any other dietary restrictions. Common allergies are dairy, nuts, and pork. Many people are vegetarians or vegans (strict vegetarians who consume no animal or dairy products).

57 Consider following a theme such as Tex-Mex or Russian food. Cookbooks often suggest complete menus.

58 Decide on your budget. Exotic foods can really add up. Perhaps simple foods served elegantly would be more realistic.

59 Plan as many dishes as possible that can be prepared or even partially prepared ahead of time.

60 Consider the capacity of your refrigerator, freezer, and oven, as well as the number of baking pans and serving dishes you have. Both factors may limit what you serve.

61 Decide whether you will begin with beverages and hors d'oeuvres.

62 Remember that a well-rounded meal includes a protein, green vegetable, another vegetable, and a starch.

63 Include different textures and colors.

64 Make flavors compatible.

65 Plan for attractive presentations such as garnishes and sauces.

66 Make sure that all the dishes that will need to go in the oven at the last minute will fit and use the same temperature setting.

67 Determine if you will need to keep things warm or cold and how you will do that.

68 **Setting your table properly**

Get in the habit of setting the table correctly every night for family dinners. You don't have to set it all out, just do what is appropriate for the meal, putting the utensils in their proper places—drinking glasses above the knives, etc. Practice proper etiquette as well. (My kids seem to display the best manners away from home so all that training must be sinking in.)

When setting my table for a dinner party, I start in the middle of each place setting, working my way to the right and then over to the left of the dinner plate. These are the steps:

Step One: The dinner plate goes in the middle. At a formal dinner, the salad is served on a plate that is placed on top of the dinner plate.

Step Two: To the right of the plate place the knife with blade facing the plate. Place the

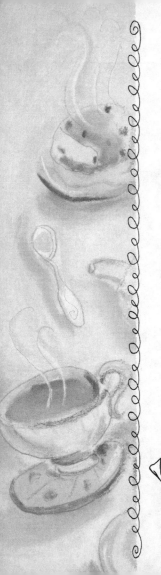

spoon next to the knife, and if soup is on the menu, put the soup spoon next to that.

Step Three: Above the knife place the water glass or goblet. If used, the wine goblet should be put to the right of the water glass.

Step Four: On the left side of the dinner plate, place forks, tines up, in the reverse order of use. That means the dessert fork should be placed next to the plate, followed by the dinner fork, with the salad fork on the outside.

Step Five: The rule of thumb is that guests will use the outermost utensils as they progress through the courses of the dinner and work their way to the innermost pieces, always keeping knives and spoons on the right and forks on the left. Place any special use silverware with that in mind. For instance, shrimp forks probably would be placed at the farthest left. Dessert spoons would be closest to the plate. Dessert utensils can also be placed horizontally above the dinner plate or brought with the dessert.

Step Six: The bread plate goes above or to the left of the forks. If you are using individual butter knives, place them across the top of the bread plates. If the dinner is less formal, the salad plate is placed above the forks instead of the bread-and-butter plate.

Step Seven: Be sure the bottom edges of all the silverware and the bottom edge of the dinner plate form a straight line. Line up all the silverware neatly alongside the plate.

✎ Involving your kids

It is never too early to train your children in the fine art of making your guests feel welcome and blessed. Planning age-appropriate chores and

activities for them will make them feel important—and your guests will be sooo charmed!
Your wonderful wee ones may be able to:

- Take wraps at the front door and put
  them away
- Set the table
- Make place cards, napkin rings, or other
  decorations
- Clean their rooms
- Help clean the house
- Do some chopping or mixing with your
  supervision in the kitchen
- Provide input on the menu. With a little
  garnishing, their favorites just might be
  company material.
- Shop with you, allowing you to teach them
  how to choose the best produce and meats
  and to compare prices
- Play background music softly while guests are
  arriving. Make those music lessons pay off!

- Refill water glasses
- Serve hors d'oeuvres and other easily
  handled dishes
- Eat with you and your guests. This is a great
  opportunity for them to consciously practice
  their manners.

Seating guests

Sometimes you need to consider carefully how
your guests will get along. In such instances,
do some "social engineering," using place cards
to make it an enjoyable event for everyone.

70 The guest of honor sits on the host's right;
the second most honored guest should sit on
hostess's right.

71 Alternating male and female guests is no longer
a hard-and-fast rule but is often more fun.

72 Make sure you mix up the guests so that extro-
verts sit next to introverts. This is one way that
you may be able to draw out your quieter guests.

73 This may be a good time to facilitate connections. For instance, seat the investor next to the entrepreneur or the single male next to available single female.

～～～～ Reality Check ～～～～

You do not want to have to worry about or fuss with your apparel when you should be caring for your guests. So although discussing what to wear when entertaining guests may seem a bit frivolous, it can prevent frustrations later on. A few suggestions:

• Avoid wearing dangling scarves, jewelry, and other items that may drag into pots or dishes as you work in the kitchen. Long sleeves can also get in the way.
• Consider wearing an attractive apron that can be removed after the cooking is completed.
• Comfortable shoes (maybe even attractive slippers) are essential, since you'll be on your feet a lot.
• Jackets may be too warm and bulky for freedom of movement and comfort.
• Also avoid wearing shirts that won't stay tucked in.

74 Some careful seating arrangements may have to be done ahead of time to prevent two best friends from talking exclusively to each other. Do not let them shift the place cards!

75 You may want to avoid placing people with strong opposing views, such as the butcher and the vegan, next to each other unless they are already good, understanding friends.

TOP TEN LIST OF THINGS *NOT* TO DO AT YOUR DINNER PARTY

Since the purpose of inviting people into your home is to bless them, you certainly do not want to insult them or in any way hurt their feelings. Your guests' comfort and sensitivities need to be respected. If you remember a time when you were offended by a hostess or fellow dinner guest then you have a good example of a bad example.

What follows is my "Top Ten List of Things *Not* to Do":

Number One: Fail to inform the guests that the party is formal or casual. (Ever been the only one in jeans in a room full of people in their Sunday best?)

Number Two: Let cats and dogs remain in the dining area. Some people have allergies. I have personally suffered ruined pants, skirts, sweaters, and hosiery from pet claws, and some painful scratches and bruises as well. Flying pets need to remain caged.

Number Three: Allow the young and hardy to rest in the best chairs while the old and infirm sit uncomfortably.

Number Four: Put a lefty between two righties on one side of the table. Lefties go on an end where they will not bump elbows with righties.

Number Five: Serve food that a guest cannot eat because of allergies, religious or other beliefs, and then not provide an alternative.

Number Six: Allow kids to get away with poor manners, either by permitting children to dominate the conversation or refusing to discipline them when they are behaving poorly.

Number Seven: Allow a guest to say things that would hurt or anger another without tactfully interfering and trying to smooth things over.

Number Eight: Gossip.

Number Nine: Put a talented guest on the spot by asking for a performance. This is especially true if your guest makes his or her living as a professional performer. Your company comes to relax, not work. Let normal friendships form

between your guests and forget that anyone could be considered more special than any other.

Number Ten: Neglect to put out extra toilet paper in the powder room.

"You see, we really ought to have a banquet at once, to celebrate this affair. It's expected of you—in fact, it's the rule."

—Badger to Toad in *The Wind in the Willows*
by Kenneth Grahame

Chapter 7
Feeding Large Crowds in Your Home

On many Friday nights at 5:30 our church's college group descends upon our home for dinner and some kind of activity. Matt, the adult leader and a well-trained cook, arrives early with dinner almost completely made. He then prepares a tossed green salad and an entrée such as Mexican chicken casserole, spaghetti, or lasagna. Dinner is served buffet-style on the kitchen countertop separating our dining room from the kitchen. Our little home gets pretty cozy when a dozen or so kids squeeze around the dining table or gather in the basement family room. For our modest home, that is a big crowd.

My sister, Sue, and her husband designed their home in Phoenix, Arizona, to accommodate a hundred or more for parties. The weather is usually perfect in the evenings, so even more people can congregate outdoors. Youth groups, Sunday school classes, class reunions, and other large gatherings have been welcome there.

Unless they are hosting a potluck, they prefer to have a caterer provide the food for crowds that number more than thirty. For their daughter's wedding reception dinner, seventy-two guests comfortably dined at round tables set up inside their home. The dinner was served from the large built-in buffet Sue designed for just such occasions when they built their home twenty years ago. A lot of what I know about preparing for big crowds I gleaned from Sue.

Most of us will not host a hundred people in our home; yet whether you are hosting a group of ten or 110, you need to think through the logistics and requirements for the event. Start a file or notebook to keep track of all you need to do. Appendix A contains a timeline to help ensure you cover each step in planning an event at the appropriate time.

76 Begin by thinking through all the details

Generally, the larger the event you are hosting, the more planning you need to do. In this chapter we'll consider buffets and potlucks, which are common ways of feeding large crowds. Regardless of whether you will serve large numbers of people at a buffet, potluck, or sit-down dinner, you will need to consider many issues up front. These may include:

Food and beverages

You need to determine what food will be served, how it will be served, and who will provide it. (Later in this chapter you'll learn some ways to prepare to serve food to large groups.)

If the expected number of guests is more than I can feed using my limited kitchen and cookware, I have the affair catered. Usually that means picking up big pans of manicotti and lasagna, salad, and bread sticks from my favorite Italian restaurant.

Dishes and silverware

For formal feasts, I try to avoid paper products. (I am not above door-to-door begging, borrowing silverware and china.) But for casual affairs disposable items require less effort and are often ideal. You may be able to delegate the purchasing and cleanup. Pretty paper products might coordinate with or inspire a theme.

Location (indoors or outdoors)

You'll need to decide whether you'll use one or both. If you'll be inside, determine whether you'll need to clear out furniture to set up additional tables. If your event will be held outside, develop a backup plan in case of inclement weather.

Seating

Forget your perfect room arrangements and showing off your beautiful furniture. Move furnishings into the garage or a nearby bedroom. Nobody will miss them. Push seating to the outer walls, remove lamps and art that sits on pedestals. When your home gets crowded, accidents can easily happen and that valuable vase will be history.

I have used my living room and family room to seat extras. One friend set a table in his spacious entry. Another uses her immense main level master suite for two additional tables.

Bathroom facilities

For more than twenty people, one powder room will be inadequate. Be prepared to share another one. Have plenty of toilet paper in a basket where the guests can see it, and put out a couple of hand towels in each facility as well. You may have to assign an assistant to check on the restrooms now and then. His or her job is to do a quick wipe-down and refill the TP basket.

Coat checking

Usually a room nearby such as a study, den, or the master bedroom works best. Assign one or two people (a great job for kids) to the task of taking wraps and putting them away. Make sure the guests know where their things are going so they can retrieve them later. When huge hoards descend, have greeters direct guests to where they can leave their coats.

In some areas of the country it is understood that everyone removes their footwear as well as their coats. Many of my friends with new white carpeting require all comers to remove their shoes. One friend hung a calligraphic sign on her front door to make sure this happens. If you want guests to remove their shoes, make sure you've made room for them on your floor or in your closet.

Parking

Clear your driveway of all cars and let your guests know if parking on the street is permis-

sible. If you expect many cars, have the courtesy to warn your neighbors. Also, encourage carpooling among your guests.

Providing directions

Remember those maps I suggested you create in chapter 2? Make lots of copies!

Name tags

These are often a good idea. You can buy packages of sticky name tags for guests to fill in when they arrive. At a reunion I attended a few years ago, a talented classmate made name tags with our old photos on them. Embarrassing, but fun.

Activities and food for children

Many parents of tiny tots own booster seats that work well. You need to communicate with any parents of little ones to make sure their needs are met.

A few years ago we had my husband's office party in our home. Children were invited. This meant that the kids needed a place to eat and the program had to be kid-friendly. Josh, Jon, and Anna hosted tables in a room separate from the adults and then led their young guests in some activities and crafts until the adults were ready to join them for the gift exchange, a silly game or two, and carols sung around the piano. It was a lot of work but it gave the adults some time away from the little ones.

Music, entertainment, or other program

If you are coordinating this with a committee or the entertainers themselves, be sure to work out space, electrical issues, and other needs ahead of time.

THE BUFFET

Whether you cook all the food yourself or the whole gang brings food to your house, serving food to the masses is often most efficiently done buffet style.

Where to serve the food

Think through traffic flow and anticipate where possible bottlenecks could occur. Locating the buffet near the kitchen is often the most convenient. Some ideas of possible serving spots:

77 A long countertop in your kitchen.

78 A desk or similar surface.

79 A piece of plywood placed over a too-small surface such as a bookshelf. Cover it with a pretty cloth and place a heavy decorative piece on top so the plywood will not topple.

80 A kitchen or dining room table, possibly shoved into a corner or against a wall. It may also be possible to place the table in the middle of the room, allowing guests to circle the entire table.

81 A sideboard or buffet table in your dining room.

82 A folding table or two set up near the kitchen or dining room.

83 Rolling carts also provide serving space.

How to serve the food

Regardless of where the food is served, the following steps will make the buffet line move smoothly.

84 Set up your buffet line in a logical order. Serving pieces and food should be set up in an order something like this:

> Dinner plates and trays if they are needed
> Main dish
> Side dishes; place salad dressings, if needed, next to salads
> Breads (and butter if not placed on tables)
> Desserts if they are being served at same time
> Silverware and napkins (if not already on tables)

85 Consider ahead of time how you will keep hot things hot and cold things cold. Keep in mind that it is not safe to have guests walk over or on electrical wires.

86 If a diner will need to use two hands to get a serving of food to his plate, make sure there is room on the buffet table to set the plate down.

87 Serve beverages at a separate location. Since spills are possible, the kitchen is often the best place.

88 If everyone will be sitting at tables, put silverware and napkins at each place and baskets of bread in the center of each table.

89 Make sure each table has salt, pepper, and butter (if needed for bread).

90 Wait until dinner has been served to set out desserts.

Keeping food the correct temperature

No matter how well you plan the way you serve the food, you and your guests will be disappointed if the food is not the right temperature.

Sometimes it is tricky keeping all the cold foods cold and the hot foods hot on a buffet. Furthermore, anytime certain foods are kept out too long, there is the possibility of food poisoning. After sixty minutes at room temperature, for instance, meats must be refrigerated.

91 Many dishes will stay cool for a while and need no chilling if they are served promptly and returned to the fridge or freezer right away. Large bowls or pans of ice keep cool foods chilled.

92 Keeping foods hot can be trickier. Electric food warmers, Crock-Pots, and other electrical devices may work. If they need to stay plugged in, arrange them so no one trips over the cords.

93 Chafing dishes are pans that sit on racks over candles. Look for these in gourmet food stores or at restaurant suppliers. I found some at my local price club. Many churches own them. Since such equipment can be pricey, ask around and see if you can borrow some of the items you need. My circle of friends freely shares everything from ice buckets to folding tables. I like to return equipment in pristine condition with a thank-you note.

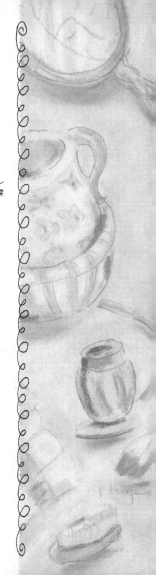

Making food easy to serve

You'll disappoint a guest when the delicious-looking chili is lukewarm; you'll frustrate him when he drops his cornbread trying to ladle out a bowl of chili with one hand and hold his plate in another.

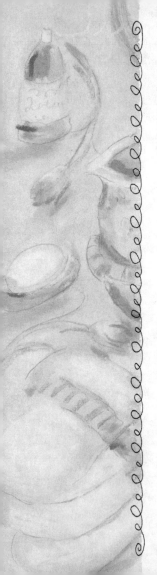

When arranging food on the buffet line where guests will serve themselves, keep these three lofty goals in mind: They should be able to do it easily 1) with one hand, 2) in one try, and 3) with no spills.

Nothing is more frustrating than trying to extract a serving of food from a pan with an inadequate utensil. It is frustrating and causes accidents. Tongs, serving spoons, ladles, spatulas, cake servers, meat forks, and salad tongs can simplify the process and are less embarrassing for uncoordinated individuals. (Oh, the messes I have made!)

∽∽∽∽∽∽ Reality Check ∽∽∽∽∽∽

The most difficult part of planning my menu is generally the main dish. Over the years, however, I've created a list of tasty options. Once I've determined that, deciding on the other dishes is easy and predictable. I add a vegetable, fresh salad, bread, and dessert. Generally I serve a light dessert with a heavy dinner and vice versa.

The following ideas will make food service easier for your guests:

94 Cut food into separate servings before you open the buffet to guests.

95 Slice meat into serving sizes.

96 Pull apart individual rolls and cut slices of bread completely.

97 If two hands will be required to extricate a single serving, leave plenty of room for people to set down their plates in front of the food.

THE POTLUCK

Potlucks. Everyone loves them: serving yourself from tables crowded with yummy food; discovering new recipes; trying to identify the mysterious spice in that casserole. Recently, however, I was reminded of what happens when you let a potluck "just happen." What was publicized as a "women's potluck luncheon" actually became a "women's dessert"! The members of my Bible study were all told to bring whatever we wanted. Well, nearly everyone felt like having dessert that day! There was one basket of rolls, one salad, and an amazing array of sweets. It was yummy—but not very satisfying for those on restricted diets. So now all the ladies at my church are firm believers in what we call the "planned potluck."

Begin planning your potluck with some consensus of what sort of meal everyone wants. Although potluck meals typically include main dishes, side dishes, breads, desserts, and beverages, some of the most interesting take a different twist. Last week our Bible study had a salad potluck to which every member brought a large salad. Another group of women might choose to create a salad bar potluck and ask each person to bring something to add to the salad. Perhaps a group of employees planning a potluck lunch around a planning meeting would decide on a sandwich bar with several varieties of sandwich meats and breads.

98 Make a potluck sign-up sheet

When you are coordinating a potluck, make a sign-up sheet that includes all pertinent information for those who will be attending:

- ☑ Occasion, date, time, place

- ☑ Name of coordinator and contact information (phone number and e-mail address)

- ☑ How many people each dish should serve
  Participants need to be reminded that appropriate serving dishes and utensils should be brought with each dish. It is not right to show up at someone's home with a bag of salad straight

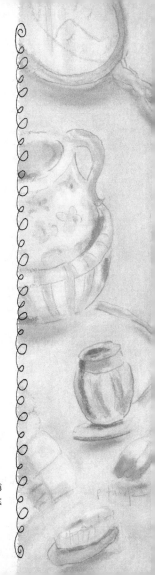

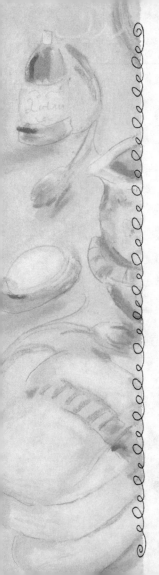

from the grocer's produce department and expect the hostess to come up with the serving bowl, serving utensils, and dressings.

☑ A list of items needed and quantity desired
Below each item include as many lines as you need to provide enough for the expected crowd. Ask people to write their phone number or e-mail address next to their name.

Do not forget salt, pepper, butter, and condiments. Cups, ice, napkins, cutlery, plates, and perhaps even soup bowls have to be brought if the hostess is not providing them.

The cleanup crew needs to be planned, as well.

When buying disposable cutlery, dishes, napkins, and cups remember to buy more than the number of people expected. Also, remember the longer the event, the more supplies you will need.

When the list is filled, you will want to have some system to remind people what they have agreed to bring. In some situations, you can post the list somewhere. Sometimes I include sticky notes with the sign-up list so each person can make himself or herself a note. If the potluck will be held in an unfamiliar location, I attach maps to the sign-up sheet. The map itself then serves as a reminder. Finally, you (or the coordinator) could mail, call, or e-mail a reminder a few days before the event.

COOKING AHEAD FOR LARGE CROWDS

When planning any large event where food will be served remember to do as much as you can as far ahead as you can.

99 Maximize your freezer

If you have access to a freezer, cook and freeze as much as you can. Besides precooked foods, you can freeze all the breads, juices, milk, butter, and margarine. Be sure to label everything.

What else can you make ahead that freezes well?

- Cookies
- Spaghetti sauce
- Most casseroles
- Pies and cakes
- Soups and stews

- Browned ground beef
- Chopped onions
- Grated cheeses
- Twice-baked potatoes
- Pizzas (I buy the kind that are all assembled and ready to bake.)
- Meatballs
- Enchiladas, burritos, and chimichangas

Of course, cooking ahead also saves stress for those times when you are anticipating houseguests—or your husband or teenage son unexpectedly comes home with a few hungry friends!

"So the children sat in their thrones . . . and that night there was a great feast in Cair Paravel, and revelry and dancing, and gold flashed and wine flowed."

—The Lion, the Witch and the Wardrobe by C. S. Lewis

Chapter 8
Special Touches for Meals

My daughter, Anna, had definite ideas about decorations for her third birthday. The operative word was *pink*. The dining-room table featured a pink tablecloth overlaid with a white lace tablecloth. Only our finest china, silver, and crystal would do. Napkins were tied with pink bows. Pink curling ribbon spiraled down from the chandelier. A bouquet of pink and white garden roses made up the centerpiece. The corners of the tablecloths were gathered together with gaudy pink bows. Everyone wore her frilliest pink dress. Grandma Janssen even wore her mink stole. Peanut butter and jelly sandwiches were cut into pretty shapes. Favorite fruits were arranged like flower petals. It was all just *too-too!*

The Janssen Five don't go all out every time we entertain, but it is fun every now and then to create "an Experience." We use whatever we have on hand to establish an ambiance that is much appreciated and enjoyed by our guests.

Usually, extravagant decorations and details fall into the nonessentials category in my life. However, when doing a theme party,

the attention to detail is what carries it off successfully. This is a great way to involve the children as well.

PLACE CARDS

Sometimes our "social engineering" requires place cards. (Watch out for card switchers!)

100 Use place cards

Sometimes place cards are another way to carry out a theme. They are also a great craft project for kids. As you work on them, keep the following in mind:

• Double-check spelling of names before you begin.
• Write each diner's name on both the front and back of the place card so the person across the table can see the name as well.
• Elegant place-card holders and place cards can be purchased. One friend has a porcelain set that she uses with wipe-off pens.

Making your own place cards

101 The simplest place card is a piece of stiff paper, like card stock, cut into about a three-inch square and folded once. (Unlined three-by-five cards make two place cards that are just begging for embellishment.)

After practicing on scrap paper, carefully write the name on the front and back. Leave the cards unadorned or decorate with stickers, freehand art, dried flowers, bows, or stamped designs.

102 Any fruit or vegetable that you can get to stand up (try slicing a bit off the bottom) can be used to anchor a toothpick holding a place card that has been glued to it. You may need to put something between the produce and the tabletop to prevent stains.

103 Collect tiny tabletop frames and insert the name or photo of each guest.

104 Use a gel pen to write names on fall leaves, votive candleholders, Christmas tree ornaments, minipillows, sachets, tiny gifts, small books, wee stuffed animals, miniature dolls, or other small toys such as Matchbox cars. They can double as party favors.

105 Write names on sugar cookies and place each in a paper muffin cup. Use shapes and colors that carry out your theme. These can double as dessert or party favors.

106 Any ball-shaped item can be forced to stand still by making a "collar" for it to stand in. A strip of paper or cardboard cut about one inch wide and six inches long with the ends then glued or stapled will hold a Christmas tree ornament, fruit, vegetable, baseball, or an egg.

107 Make your napkin holder do double duty by either writing directly on it or attaching a name tag with decorative ribbon.

Napkin folding

While browsing in my local bookstore the other day, I discovered not just one but several books solely devoted to the art of napkin folding. My first reaction was "Who has time!" and my next was "Someone needs to get a life." Complicated napkin folding definitely falls into the nonessential category. A napkin folded in eighths to make a rectangle or triangle and then placed on the plate, to the left of the forks, or under the forks is attractive enough. But if you want to add one more special thematic detail and have the time, by all means do a fancy napkin fold. Some consider it an art form.

Napkin art can be completed days ahead of time and stored in a closet until it is time to set the table. Some of these folds require a little

practice and fussing. This is another way to get the kids involved.

Large (about twenty inches square), starched linen napkins lend themselves best to fancy folding. I will start with the easiest first; the final three examples are fairly complicated.

108 The fan

Fold the napkin once to form a long rectangle. Fold it accordion style, like you would a paper fan and then push it into a napkin ring. With the napkin ring near one end you have a fan, with it in the middle you have a double fan effect. Or forget the napkin ring and fold the fan in half and place it in the goblet.

109 The scroll

Fold the napkin once and then begin to roll it up at one end. Keep it together with a napkin ring.

110 The V

With the napkin unfolded, begin rolling it up from one corner, moving diagonally toward the opposite corner. Fold in half and put it in a goblet or a napkin ring.

111 The double flower

With the napkin unfolded, begin folding the napkin accordion style, starting at one corner and ending at the corner diagonally across from it. Fold it in half and put it in a napkin ring with most of the ends on top and the folded end just sticking down about two inches below the napkin ring. Splay the two pleated ends a bit to form large "flowers."

112 The pocket

Fold the napkin into quarters. Put all the unfolded corners on the upper left. Take the

top layer of the napkin from the upper left and fold it down an inch and then fold it under two more times. Carefully lift the whole napkin and fold both the left and right sides under. The result should be a pocket on the front in which you can place silverware or a flower.

113 The fleur-de-lis

Fold the napkin into a large triangle with the fold on top, then follow these steps:

Step One: Take both top corners (points) and fold them down to the lower point of the triangle. You have formed a diamond.

Step Two: Take the top point of the diamond and fold it down to about one inch from the bottom point resulting in an imperfect triangle. While that top point is still in

your fingers, fold it up to meet the top edge of your triangle.

Step Three: Now carefully turn the whole thing over and fold the two side points toward the middle, folding the triangle into thirds. Insert one of the side points into the other. This will be the back of the napkin.

Step Four: Now you can stand the napkin up. On the front of the napkin, take the two upper points and fold them down to make the

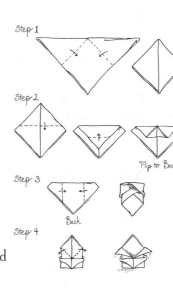

Step 1

Step 2

Flip to Back

Step 3

Back

Step 4

petals of the iris (fleur-de-lis). One solid
point should remain standing.

114 Keep it simple

True confession time: I think a fancy fold
could detract from the beauty of my napkin
holders (how's that for rationalizing away
extra work!). All I generally do is fold the
napkin in eighths to make a triangle or rectangle and place it under the fork, folded side on
the far left side. Sometimes I use a decorative
napkin holder, insert a napkin, and place it
on the center of the dinner plate.

Napkin rings and holders

Fancy folding isn't necessary if the napkin
is already dressed up with a whimsical, elegant,
or thematic napkin ring. Anything long,
skinny, and bendable
can be tied around
a napkin.

115 In addition to every imaginable kind of ribbon
and yarn, I have seen shoelaces, raffia, twine,
rope, strips of fabric, silk flowers on stems,
Christmas tree garland, lace, pearls, leather,
hair scrunchies, and elastic beaded bracelets
created into napkin rings. Use your resources
and imagination to make your own.

116 Look around to see what you have that could
be used to create the rings. My crafty sister,
Sue, made some beautiful ones for me by drying
the lovely red roses she grows and gluing them
to tiny vine wreaths. They are gorgeous and I
look for excuses to use them.

117 A few years ago I used gold French ribbon
(it has wire in the edges) to form rings. First I
rolled up the napkins and then I tied the ribbon
around them, creating bows on top. I am still
using these for special occasions, spiffing them
up each time because they get a little out of
shape in storage.

CENTERPIECES

You can spend a fortune on a flowery centerpiece. Anyone can go to a florist and order an arrangement. However, it is not necessary to blow your budget here. The purpose of a centerpiece is simply to dress up the middle of the table without obstructing eye contact between guests who sit across from each other. I like to be creative, follow a theme, and save money by assembling my own centerpiece.

118 Monochromatic centerpiece

It requires amazingly little effort to set a classy-looking table. A table set in all white—tablecloth, china, napkins, centerpiece, and clear crystal—is as elegant as you can get. Choose one color plus white and you have a smash hit as well. I have more ideas too!

Plant centerpieces

119 Select your container, such as a bowl, planter, vase, or basket. Secure some florist foam in the bottom. Snip greenery and flowers growing in your own backyard. (A variety of textures and colors will make the centerpiece interesting.) Stand the various plants in the foam. Experiment with shape, texture, and size. Beware of flowers with strong scents.

120 For an easier plant-based centerpiece, simply pull in a potted plant from outdoors or move

⟿ Reality Check ⟿

Sometimes ambiance can best be created or defined by a theme. Try using one of the following simple ideas— or let it spark your own creativity!

- When serving ethnic food it makes sense to add a few touches to the décor that emphasize that ethnicity. Use a red-checkered tablecloth when serving lasagna; at a Tex-Mex dinner, use red bandanas for napkins.
- Try a seasonal theme, using fresh flowers, fall leaves, or snow globes.
- Look to your guest of honor for inspiration. At a dinner party honoring some authors, I made their books part of the centerpiece collages.

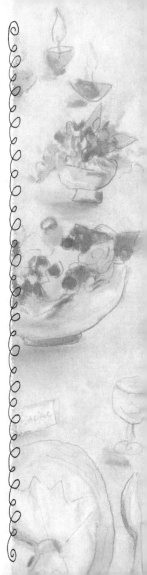

a small houseplant to the table. Add floral picks for added interest.

Object-based centerpieces

121 Use a clear container to show off pinecones, Christmas tree ornaments, fruits, vegetables, nuts, or something else that fits your theme.

122 Heap an opaque container such as a bowl or basket with the same kind of items so that they are clearly visible over the top. Crumpled newspaper or Spanish moss put in the bottom of the container lifts them closer to the top of the container.

123 Rather than a container, you can artfully arrange a collection of objects in the middle of the table. Follow a theme by grouping together silver, china, small art objects, fruit, nuts, vegetables, confetti, toys, dolls, stuffed animals, books, or whatever you can pull together. Let your imagination run wild as you hunt for stuff in your closets, cupboard, basement, attic, and yard. Or work in the opposite direction and decide if a group of your hidden treasures inspires a common theme or color. Anchor the grouping with a tray, a square of fabric, a piece of tulle, a table runner, or another foundation. To add height, consider arranging your items on a cake dish with a pedestal.

Some obvious themes are seasons, holidays, and different cultures or countries. Dig a little deeper into your imagination and you may come up with an era, color, collection, hobby, season of life, occupation, antique, television show, movie, or pastime—or even a game—motif. Have fun with it!

Candle centerpieces

For an evening dinner party, you may decide to include candles as part of the centerpiece. This is a great time to use the silver candlestick holders you received as a wedding gift, but for something different try one of the following ideas.

124 You can make almost any fruit or vegetable into a candleholder by using an apple corer to create a hole. If the produce is tipsy, slice off a bit of the bottom and place it on a plate or saucer to protect your table.

125 You can add the drama of candlelight without the typical tapers by using tea or votive candles in attractive holders or custard cups. (Not all cups can withstand the heat, so select carefully.) Candleholders can be embellished with bows, paint, and floral material.

126 My current centerpiece is an antique silver-plated tray (a beat-up family heirloom) on which I've set a bunch of pillar and votive candles. My family calls it "our fireplace." Small embellishments change with the seasons. Last Christmas I added twigs of holly. Fall leaves and nuts preceded that.

Whenever using candles in your centerpieces, keep a few things in mind:

- Keep flammables away from the candle flames and the hot dripping wax.
- Light the candles as everyone is being seated. Never leave them unattended.
- When or if the party moves to another room, snuff out the candles.
- Keep the flame level either below or above eye level. Otherwise your guests may find it uncomfortable to look through them to make eye contact with other guests.
- Use a candlesnuffer or a willing volunteer (usually a man wanting to show off) to pinch out the flames to prevent flying candle wax and avoid wax stains on linens.
- Do not use scented candles around food.

A great deal of the taste of foods relies on the smell. The scent of a candle will interfere with the enjoyment of your meal.

Decorations

When a girlfriend of mine returned from a mission trip to Russia, we invited her and other friends over for borsch and a recap of the trip. To set the stage, we used the table linens and teacups Al picked up in Russia fourteen years ago. We also played a Tchaikovsky recording in the background. We all felt very Russian!

To create a mood, set the scene, and crank up the atmosphere. Let yourself go wild with your theme as you use what you have to decorate for an event. Brainstorm with your friends and family or go to a party store for ideas. Some of my ideas for jazzing up an occasion include:

127 Drape tulle or fabric over furniture.

128 Go on-line to find printable images and then attach them to construction paper "frames" before taping the artwork to the walls in symmetrical groupings.

129 Weave Christmas tree lights through the branches and leaves of plants and tape them around doors and windows.

130 Cover lampshades with squares of translucent tissue paper or fabric.

131 Hang things like toys, ribbons, jewelry, loops of fabric, silk vines, and stars from the chandelier.

132 Decorate dining chairs, especially the guest of honor's.

133 Use tempera paints to brush a scene onto a window.

134 Dim the lights and ignite dozens of votive candles.

Attractive food garnishes

Even the simplest garnish will enhance the attractiveness of a dish. It is worth the trouble to give even a commonplace dish a gourmet touch.

135 Soups may be enhanced with a dollop of sour cream, a sprinkle of grated cheese, or croutons.

136 Carrot curls are easy to make ahead of time and really dress up a salad. Use a vegetable parer to make long, thin pieces. Curl up the pieces, poke a toothpick in them to keep them together, and store them in ice water until ready for use. Remove the toothpicks before serving.

137 Celery flowers are also easy to make in advance. Cut celery into even sticks of about three to five inches. Slit both ends into lots of narrow strips that reach almost half way down the sticks. Place them in iced water in the fridge. The ends will magically curl up.

138 Make a cucumber flower by running fork tines lengthwise down the sides of the vegetable before slicing it.

139 Grate some cheese on top of the vegetable or entree.

140 Sprinkle on a couple tablespoons of chopped green onions or other fresh herbs.

141 Reserve a bit of one ingredient in a recipe and then dribble it over the top of the finished dish.

142 Some foods lend themselves easily to use as garnishes because of their attractive color, texture, and taste. Fresh vegetables that work well are parsley, diced chives, cilantro, mustard greens, red onion slices, mushrooms, bell pepper, and baby carrots. Some of these will look best as a ring around the meat on a meat platter. Others will be more attractive if artfully placed on top of food.

143 Desserts can be dressed up with fresh berries, sliced fresh fruit, flavored syrups, chopped nuts, whipped cream, a sprinkle of chocolate chips, a dash of cinnamon, a maraschino cherry, or grated chocolate. Just make sure the garnish is compatible with the dessert.

144 Look through your illustrated cookbooks. They often picture dishes enhanced with garnishes and may even include directions on making additional garnishes.

"Happy hearts and happy faces,
Happy play in grassy places—
That was how, in ancient ages,
Children grew to kings and sages."

—*Good and Bad Children* by Robert Louis Stevenson

Chapter 9
Birthday Parties for Kids

For her fourteenth birthday, my daughter, Anna, went Hollywood and had an "After the Oscars Party." Our home was transformed into a stylish restaurant with framed "autographed" photos (found on the Internet) all over the walls where our art once hung, strings of white Christmas lights everywhere, fancy foods artistically arranged on silver platters, and sparkling apple cider served in champagne glasses. The dozen girls designed evening gowns using rolls of toilet paper, played charades, and watched past Oscar-winning movies. We constructed our own little golden statuettes, and each guest received one based on her performances and participation in the evening's games. We did glamorous makeovers and used the digital camera so the girls could take home their "after" photos. The girls had a ball. And it didn't cost much to make it all happen.

Some parents seem

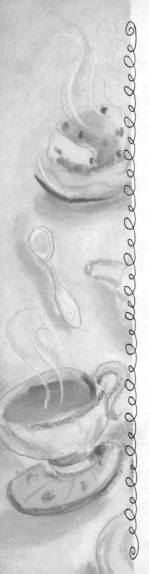

to compete to see who can put on the most elaborate and expensive birthday party for their child. Personally, I refuse to play that game. The Janssen Five have always enjoyed the challenge of living within our modest means but we do like to have a good time. Thankfully, funds do not equal fun.

Not yet convinced that you, too, can pull off a birthday party that makes your child happy without breaking your budget? Consider my ideas for making the next birthday party the best ever. All that your child will need are some friends, a few age-appropriate activities, crowd-pleasing food, and a happy heart.

The guests

145 The younger the crowd, the shorter the party should be. An hour is sufficient for tiny tots. Planning and entertaining for two hours is plenty for any age!

146 In general, limit the number of guests to the child's age. When my daughter turned five she could extend invitations to five friends. Fewer is even better!

147 Carefully consider the mix of guests. It's best if they all know one another from school, church, or some other activity. If you want to include someone else, it is wise to consider how comfortable that person will be if she doesn't know anyone besides your child. You may want to invite at least two from each set of friends.

148 Structure the party for your guests. Free-for-alls can quickly develop into disasters.

149 A party is a perfect opportunity for the birthday child to learn the responsibilities involved in being a thoughtful, competent host. Prior to party time, practice introductions and discuss how to make everyone feel welcome and included. Remind your child that every gift should be received graciously. Although

he may be the center of attention, his attention should be on everyone else. Thank-you notes should go out within a week.

Other party details

150 The time of day will determine whether you'll need to serve a meal at the party.

151 The easiest time for a party is midafternoon when only dessert is expected. Additionally, you will have all morning to prepare and all evening to recuperate.

152 Plan the theme, games, and activities with the birthday honoree. He or she may have some terrifically creative ideas.

153 Immediately engage the guests with a game, craft, or activity as soon as they arrive.

154 Think neat and simple when planning your menu. Cookies, muffins, juice bags, granola bars, and milkshakes are tidy alternatives to the traditional ice cream, cake, and punch.

155 In many parts of the country, goodie bags—paper or cellophane bags filled with small toys and candy—are routinely given out to guests. To avoid spending big bucks at your drugstore the night before the party, decide early whether you will give them and, if so, what will be in them. The theme of the party may give you direction.

Some years I had my birthday boy decorate brown lunch bags. One year I sewed simple drawstring bags for little girls. Bulk candy

Reality Check

- Everyday dishes hold up better than disposable products.
- Juice bags are neater than juice served in cups but more expensive.
- Avoid serving drinks that stain, such as orange juice, red fruit punch, Kool-Aid, and colas. Apple juice and lemon-lime soda do not stain.
- Serve non-messy finger foods indoors. Save sloppy sticky stuff for outside.

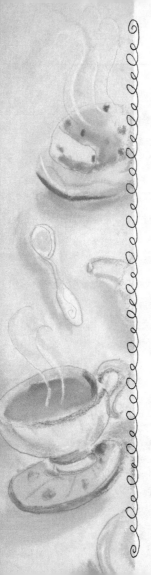

makes a cheap filler. At a pirate party we used gold-foil coins.

156 Consider recruiting a helper—perhaps an older sibling or another parent—to serve as your assistant at the party, helping with crowd control, cleanup, and photography.

157 Make shopping lists for groceries, decorations, goodie bags, games, and activities. (See my ideas for each of these in this chapter.)

158 Make a schedule to help you determine when to shop, do any activity or game preparations, clean house, call guests who have not replied, decorate, and prepare food. Refer to the lists in appendix C to make sure all bases are covered.

PARTY VENUES

159 Business party packages

Parties outside the home are popular. Many of our local businesses cater to the children's birthday-party clientele. Many require only minimal planning—and cash. They offer package deals that cover combinations of services such as a party room, activities, decorations, cake, punch, and cleanup. In our area, birthday parties can center around miniature golf, gymnastics, ceramics painting, swimming, baseball, bowling, lunch at a tea room, scrapbooking, laser tag, video games, open gym, amusement-park rides, martial arts, tourist attractions, museums, and historical homes. Check your local favorites.

160 Party at the park

The easiest and probably the least expensive party, weather permitting, is a party at a public park or playground. In our city, if you want to rent a pavilion, it has to be reserved months ahead of time, but if all you need is a picnic table or a place to spread a picnic blanket, a public park gives your party plenty of acres to play in. No housecleaning is required!

Load up the car ahead of time and pack light. Remember to bring the party food, serving pieces, a picnic blanket or tablecloth, some disposable wet cloths for washing up, paper towels, a first-aid kit, and some sports equipment. Keep the menu simple. Disposable plates, cups, napkins, and forks are easiest but have a tendency to blow away if it is windy. If you use plastic dinnerware for patio dining or camping, bring it instead. Of course, if you bring only finger foods and juice boxes or bags, you will not need plates, cups, or utensils.

You won't need crafts or highly organized games at a park. Depending on the age of the crowd, you can just let the kids frolic at the playground or bring sports equipment and let them play softball, kickball, Frisbee golf, lawn games, or basketball. An older crowd might enjoy a hike to some interesting destination.

161 Party at home

If you're budget-conscious or your child has a winter birthday, you may choose to celebrate at home. Decide where to hold the party, whether inside on the main level or in your garage, basement, patio, or yard. If the party is inside, clear away valuables and breakables.

When my children were young they liked to have parties based on a theme. This often depended on their latest interest, such as the Olympics or Peter Pan's pirates. Some other ideas for your kids' parties:

- Any sport
- Cheerleading—ask a high school cheer-leader to come and teach cheers
- A favorite cartoon character
- A favorite movie character

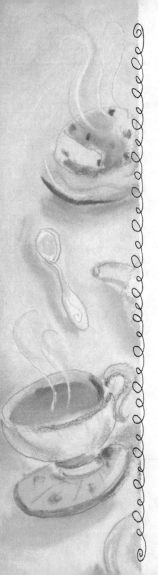

- Makeovers, beauty parlor, spa
- "Beach" party or luau
- Picnic—inside or out, in season or not
- Christmas in summer
- Another country or culture
- Hat party
- Circus
- Zoo
- A craft, such as sewing, woodworking, painting, sidewalk chalk, modeling clay, wire sculptures, flower arranging, puppet making, T-shirt art
- Adventure—safari, space, *Star Trek,* ocean exploration, camping, treasure island, pirates, cowboys
- An era—the Middle Ages, colonial times, the future
- A hobby—scrapbooking, star gazing, Lego building, hiking, gardening, cooking
- A favorite book or series—*Little House on the Prairie,* the Hardy Boys, *Little Women, The Lion, the Witch and the Wardrobe, The Hobbit, The Wind in the Willows*
- What is going on in your child's life right now? Plan a theme around it.

MAKING THE PARTY SPECIAL

The more enticing the invitation, the more intense the response.

162 **Homemade invitations**

Crank up the enthusiasm with homemade thematic invitations. Choose a motif from your theme and let your imagination go wild. The birthday child should be involved from the start. *Participation is more important than perfection.* Some ideas if you'd like to make your invitations:

- Use interesting paper for the outside of the invitations: scrapbooking paper, gift wrap, brown

paper bag, newspapers, colorful Sunday comics, maps, photos, copies of book illustrations. Glue or staple plain paper inside with all the important info written on it.

- Embellish with 3-D details such as beads, string, ribbons. (If you plan to mail your invitations, you'll need to consider what will hold up during the mailing process.)
- Design with stickers, stamps, or calligraphy.
- Cut invitations into simple shapes that go with your theme.
- Remember: if you have a computer, you have art.

163 Sending invitations

Invitations need to be bought or made and sent out two to four weeks before the party. Include the name of the birthday person, date, time it begins and ends, location, phone number, and RSVP deadline. Also include any special instructions. For instance, if the party includes water activities, guests need to be reminded to wear their swimsuits and to bring towels. Formal tea parties should note that dress is "Sunday special."

Decorations

Like homemade invitations, decorations are not essential to a successful party but they do enhance the total experience. Again, get the birthday person involved. It is a great way to channel the energy of an excited youngster. Artwork does not have to be perfect to create the desired ambiance. Mine your household's resources to follow your theme. Clear out your usual décor and make over your party place!

164 Cardboard can be cut and painted to create swords, animals, crowns, and other props.

165 Large rolls of paper are useful for making large figures, forests, castle walls, underwater

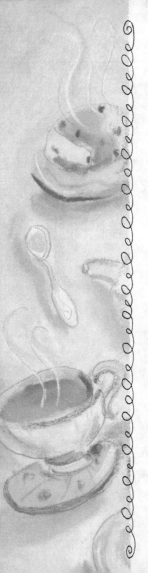

landscapes, or any environment and props that can be taped to walls. I used to buy the ends of newsprint rolls at our local newspaper office.

166 Ribbons, bows, lace, tulle, flowers, and doilies used liberally from the front door to the chandelier create a very feminine ambiance.

167 Toys, stuffed animals, and other types of props that you already own can also be used to decorate the table, front door, and chandelier, or to dress up a corner.

168 Fabric—leopard's spots to lace—from your tablecloths, sheets, or the fabric store can make a big impact.

Games

Many traditional kids' games can be creatively tweaked to go along with many themes. Just change the name of the game and rethink the props, and you have a theme-specific game.

169 **Games for preschoolers**
- Follow the Leader (This is especially fun when led by an older sibling or teen helper.)
- London Bridge
- Ring around the Rosy
- Here We Go 'Round the Mulberry Bush (Make up verses like, "This is the way we wiggle our toes, wiggle our toes, wiggle our toes . . ." Change the list of activities to fit your theme.)
- Simon Says
- Mother May I?
- Red Light, Green Light
- Farmer in the Dell
- Hokey Pokey
- Pin the Tail on the Donkey. Any creature will work. Draw a big one on a large piece of paper and make enough "tails" for everyone.
- Assign each guest a noise to make that goes with a character or noisy object such as a

train from a story that you will read aloud. Every time a character or that noisy object is mentioned, that designated guest does his thing.

170 Games for school-age kids

- Red Rover
- Statues
- Three-legged races
- Relay races
- Freeze Tag
- Tug of War
- Dodgeball
- Wheelbarrow races
- Limbo
- Obstacle course
- Musical Chairs
- Charades
- Name that Tune
- Twenty Questions
- Telephone

- Dress up with toilet paper: Divide the kids into teams of three or four. One child is chosen to be the model. Each team goes to a separate and private place. Their goal is to make the model look like a fairy-tale creature, animal, or whatever your theme suggests using the toilet paper wrapped around the model. You will need lots of cheap toilet paper, clear tape, and a camera to record all the creations.

- Musical dress up: Have the partygoers sit in a large circle. The players pass along a big bag (pillowcases work well) full of costume items from person to person as music plays. When the music stops, whoever is holding the bag has to close his eyes and pull out the first thing he touches in the bag and then put it on. When all the kids are decked out and the bag is empty, take a picture of the group and/or individuals. You will need a collection of costume items such as hats, scarves,

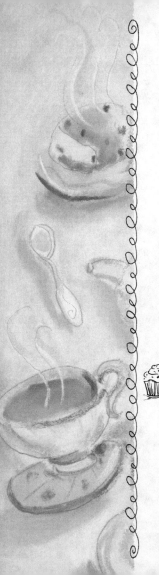

gaudy costume jewelry, capes, boots, long swishy skirts, gloves, crowns, big shirts, long gowns, bathrobes, belts, sashes, ties, boas, shawls, and such. You may want to create cardboard armor, swords, crowns, and magic wands to include in the bag. Choose some lively music and have a boom box ready to go.

• Decorate cupcakes or cookies: Partygoers can eat them then or take some home. Sugar cookies can be cut into all sorts of shapes to suit your theme.

• Alphabet game: "I am going to (thematic destination) and I am taking (something that begins with the letter A)." The next person repeats what the first person said and then adds something that begins with the next letter in the alphabet. The longer the game continues, the harder it is to remember what all the previous people said!

• Birthday person's word game: Make words out of the birthday person's full name. Example: From "John Roy Jones" you can make "son," "sore," "honey," "nose," and many more.

• Remember what's on the tray: Present twenty things on a tray and allow kids to look at it for sixty seconds before removing it. Kids write down as many as they can remember.

• Adventure story: Write and illustrate an original story about the friends at the party embarking together on an adventure. Have illustrated storybooks around for inspiration.

• Tall tales: Begin by starting a thematically correct tall tale that includes the birthday person and stops at some exciting moment. Then ask another person to continue it.

Around it goes until everyone has had a turn to add to the adventures. The last person has to make everyone live happily ever after.

THAT SOMETHING EXTRA . . .

Slumber parties take a lot more planning because your guests will be staying so much longer.

171 Slumber parties

Make sure your guests' parents know when they are expected to pick up their kids the next day so you can get some rest! The invitation should also include a list of what they need to bring, such as a sleeping bag, pillow, and toiletries. Although you will have a home phone number for contacting, when guests RSVP or are dropped off, it's a good idea to ask for their parents' cell phone number (if they have one) in case of an emergency.

Plan on serving an evening meal, snacks all

evening, and breakfast the next morning. Simple is best. Besides pizza, I have found that spaghetti (with the sauce served separately) is acceptable to even the pickiest eaters. I serve a green salad and warm French bread with it. Keep foods confined to a certain area if you are afraid of staining carpets or furniture, or serve foods and drinks that do not stain.

At bedtime plug in a few night-lights throughout your home so your guests can get a drink of water or visit the rest room without hurting themselves. Try to keep all the guests sleeping in one area. You may have to remove some furniture.

We aim to have all the slumberers bedded down for the night in the TV room by 11 P.M. and then we show a quiet movie until they fall asleep. Our young guests are firmly but kindly informed as to the exact time when lights will be turned out and all will be perfectly quiet—and they are reminded again every thirty or sixty minutes thereafter . . . or until parents or kids fall asleep.

You will have to make sure everyone is out of bed, dressed, fed, and packed up with their stuff waiting by the front door before pickup time. Make breakfast as simple as possible. A variety of bagels and cream cheese spreads served with orange juice and milk is almost effortless. Any sweet breakfast bread like doughnuts or coffeecake is well received and easy to serve. If you have a good blender you can combine fruits, juices, ice cream, or sherbets to create nutritious, great-tasting fruit smoothies.

172 Treasure hunts

My kids enjoy treasure hunts. They don't care that the prizes are just bags of cheap candy. Our last treasure hunt was held at my daughter's "Got My Braces Off!" party last year, but the idea works equally well at birthday parties.

Anna's seventh-grade girlfriends had a blast trying to figure out my clues. We divided the gang into four groups of three by pulling names out of a hat to prevent any ill feelings. Then I handed each bunch their first clue. Every group had a different set of clues leading them to a cache of their goodie bags. I color-coded the hunt so the teams would recognize their clues and prizes by the right color. Sometimes the Reds would come across a Blue clue and they knew to leave it alone.

Since it was a beautiful spring day the game took place outside. The clues took the girls all over our eighth of an acre. In fact, I purposely had them travel as much and as far as possible to burn off excess energy and make the game more challenging. The Red team's clues went something like this:

Clue #1: If you sang with tweet, tweet, tweets, this is where you'd find good eats. (They found their clue #2 taped to the bottom of the birdfeeder in the backyard.)

Clue #2: A towering lamp can really shine and light up the lane of Nevermind. Search it high, search it low, but find the clue before you go. (Clue #3 was taped on the streetlight in front of our home, as high as I could reach while standing on a short stepladder. The girls had to help each other reach it.)

Clue #3: I can carry a cup and plate; I can seat a group of eight. I have four legs, no arms, no mind, but I do hide a clue to find. (Clue #4 was taped to the underside of the table on the back deck.)

Clue #4: Magazines, bills, and catalogs too. You know where to view the clue. (Clue #5 was in the mailbox.)

Clue #5: Geraniums of red and pink may hide a little treat, I think. (Behind the pots of geraniums on the back deck they discovered their goodie bags.)

Your clues can be as obvious or as puzzling as you like depending on the age and abilities of the hunters. My kids began enjoying treasure hunts as soon as they were able to read the clues. As they got older the clues became more obscure and the hiding places tougher to find. The more clues you hide, the longer the game will take. You are limited only by the size of your property and your imagination.

"'Tis more blessed to give than to receive; for example, wedding presents."

—H. L. Mencken (1880-1956)

Chapter 10
Bridal and Baby Showers

Twenty-six years have passed but I remember it like it was yesterday. Many of my closest girlfriends and relatives all gathered to bless *me!* I do not recall the gifts or the games at my wedding shower, but I do savor the memory of feeling so very happily loved.

The purpose of this occasion is to get friends and family together to shower gifts on the guest of honor. It is our culture's way of helping out a young bride or mother while sharing in the joyous occasion. If you have a shower to coordinate, the party planning list in appendix D will

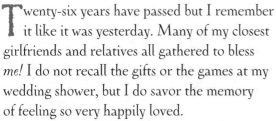

be invaluable. If you expect a big crowd, read chapter 7 to get ideas about how to handle it all.

Putting together a shower for a friend can be as simple or complicated as you want to make it. When my girlfriend was expecting a daughter, everything at her baby shower was pink— invitations, plates, napkins, cups, forks, cake, and punch. She had registered at a local department store so we could all help her put together a charming nursery. The pink nursery theme was pretty simple to carry out at her party.

One of the easiest gift theme showers to

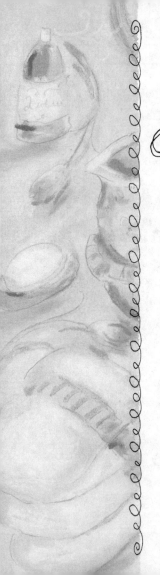

carry out is the kind where you invite your favorite representative from a company like Tupperware, PartyLite, or Pampered Chef to present a party for the honoree. The representative provides the shower invitations for the hostess to send. At the party everyone is given a gift registry that has been premade by the bride-to-be. Guests do their shopping at the party. (Sometimes they buy a little something for themselves too.) Using a theme to direct the gift giving and decorating is just one way to organize a shower.

You do not have to have a gift theme for your party; most showers I have attended do not. In fact, you do not even have to have a color scheme, although it adds a sense of style. Most discount, party, and drugstores carry coordinated party goods that will give your shower an instant color scheme and motif. Everything from the invitations to the cake can be purchased in coordinating colors and theme.

Are you on a tight budget? Use the dishes and linens you own. The first baby shower I ever gave had a Noah's Ark theme. I borrowed my kids' stuffed animal collections to use as decorations. The homemade cake was made to look like an ark. Disposable partyware was beyond my limited budget so I used the dishes, cups, forks, and napkins I had. It all came together beautifully. Most importantly, the mother-to-be was gloriously blessed by her many friends.

Reality Check

While handling all the details of the shower itself, don't forget to make those arrangements that will help the bride- or mom-to-be remember this special day. Be sure to line up a photographer, as well as someone to record the gifts and the names of the givers.

Invitations

If you have time to do more than purchase ready-made invitations, get creative. Remember, the more enticing the invitation, often the better the response. In the planning stages, decide on a theme and then design unique invitations around that theme. Your computer and resourcefulness make anything possible. Some ideas:

173 Cut invitations into a simple shape related to the theme

174 Attach ribbons, bows, buttons, fabric scraps, scraps of pretty paper, yarn, embroidery floss, beads, sticks, sand, or candy (Keep in mind what will mail well.)

175 Add further interest by using interesting paper; punching holes in a thematic design; or adding stamped designs, stickers, or photos

176 Be sure the invitation delivers all pertinent information: guest of honor, theme, date, time, party address, maps or directions, names of hosts, phone numbers, and a firm RSVP date. Also include names of stores where the guest of honor has registered.

BRIDAL SHOWERS

Consider suggesting a gift-giving theme to your guests. This may be especially helpful for the bride who is having multiple showers.

177 **Gift-giving themes**
- Gift certificates
- Storage items
- Secondhand treasures (heirlooms or antiques)
- Tupperware, Pampered Chef, candles, baskets, or other home party sales
- Christmas decorations
- Make a quilt
- Cleaning supplies
- Garden
- Library

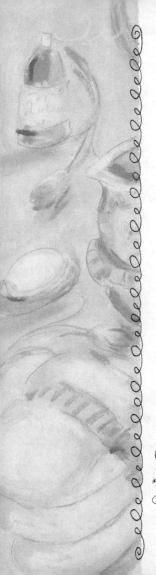

- Pantry
- Tools
- Hobby
- Common interest couple enjoys
- Spa items
- Sports
- Pictures (frames, film, albums)

Activities

178 Ask each guest to write down a favorite family tradition on a three-by-five card.

179 Ask each guest to bring a tip on romance to share.

180 Ask each guest to contribute a favorite recipe.

181 Complete a scrapbooking project.

182 Hold an outdoor barbecue.

183 Put on a Victorian tea.

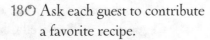

Décor

184 Use lots of framed wedding photos—ask for help on this!

185 With a little creativity, you can turn many things into a "bride and groom." Use white tulle, fabrics, and ribbons to made brides; black paper, felt, or fabric to make grooms.

186 Display photo collages of the bride and groom.

187 Go wild with your theme! Incorporate your motif, color scheme, or gift-giving theme into your centerpiece, decorations, cake design, activities, and even the party favors if they are used.

188 Devotional ideas

When hosting a shower, I often prepare a brief devotional to present. Some Scriptures to inspire you:

Genesis 2:20-25 (the first marriage)
Proverbs 18:22 (the value of a good wife)

Proverbs 31:10-31 (the job description)

Hosea 2:19-20 (the covenant)

John 2:1-11 (Jesus at a wedding feast)

1 Corinthians 13:1-13 (what true love looks like)

Titus 2:3-5 (where older women are admonished to teach younger women how to be good wives)

Baby Showers

Coordinate with the mother-to-be, who may be planning motifs and colors for her nursery. Possible themes:

189 Gift-giving themes
- Gift certificates
- Coupons—homemade (for baby-sitting, meals, etc.) or otherwise (diapers, formula, etc.)
- Children's books
- Nursery decorations
- Homemade frozen dinners
- Spa items or other gifts to spoil the new mom
- Clothing
- Diapers
- The unglamorous necessities

Activities

190 Ask guests to write down their best parenting tip or advice on a three-by-five card for the new mom.

191 Ask guests to bring their favorite family tradition on a three-by-five card.

192 Make a quilt.

193 Ask guests to write out and complete this statement: "What I said I'd never do but now it makes sense" on a three-by-five card. These are fun to read and share!

Décor

194 Incorporate baby booties, children's books, dolls, stuffed animals, or other toys into the decorations.

195 Be inspired by the chosen nursery decor.

196 Drape yards of tulle around the room to create a dreamy atmosphere.

197 Use baby blankets for tablecloths.

198 Hang small baby items from the chandelier.

199 Devotional ideas

The Bible is full of references to children. You might choose to focus on one of the miraculous babies:

Genesis 21:1-7 (Isaac)
Exodus 2:1-10 (Moses)
1 Samuel 1 (Samuel)
1 Chronicles 22:6-13 (Solomon)
Luke 1:5-23 (John the Baptist)

Other Scriptures show how our Lord values children:

Psalm 127:3-5
Matthew 19:13-1-5
Luke 18:15-17

Still others explain that God knows us before our birth:

Psalm 22:10
Psalm 71:6
Psalm 139:13-16
Isaiah 44:1-5
Jeremiah 1:5

Does all this talk about artistic invitations and clever decorations scare you off? Then make it simple. The true necessities for a successful shower are simply a generous heart and loving friends. Just send out store-bought invitations or e-mail them, pick up a cake at the bakery, brew some coffee, and clean up the living room.

"Like Christmas—in the mountains we shoot rifle-guns up chimneys and blow up tree stumps to celebrate."

—Mr. Pentland, the mailman, explaining mountain Christmas traditions to Christy in *Christy* by Catherine Marshall

Chapter 11
Christmas and New Year's Eve

Twenty-nine years ago my parents seemed to thoroughly enjoy their new empty-nest status—until Christmas, that is. They wanted us all to return to the nest. And we did. Like our parents, we couldn't stand to see friends stranded on Christmas, so we all brought guests. I brought my roommate. My brother, Andy, brought his best friend, and so on. Everyone was welcomed into the fold like long-lost relatives. My parents are happiest, I think, when their home is full to overflowing with friends and family. And Christmas is a festive excuse to invite both friends and new acquaintances to your home!

These days, the whole of December "'tis the season to be jolly-busy"! Use my planning list in appendix A to prepare for anything from the quiet family celebration to the big company Christmas party. Since December can be such a hurried, harried time, you may wish to review the basic organizational principles outlined in chapter 2: Do as much ahead of time as possible. Plan. Delegate. Communicate. Remember, it is not about *you*. Now

consider these helpful hints for heavenly hospitality during the holidays.

CHRISTMAS PARTIES

With the home smelling of evergreens and "Joy to the World" lifting our spirits, it is easy to get into the party mood. But don't wait until the decorations are up to plan one! Sometime in the fall begin thinking about what kind of holiday party you would like to have, whom you would invite, and when you can fit it into your busy schedule. I cannot help you determine the date, but I do have ideas about what to do and whom to invite!

Most of us will be involved with a few parties organized by the company we work for or organizations to which we belong. Is one of these events something you could host? We usually find a way to get together with our close friends as well. But let us not forget that Christmas is the perfect time to reach out to the lonely, the hurting, and especially the unsaved. What kinds of parties can you host that would bring together many of the people you care for? A few come to mind: the cookie exchange, caroling party, craft-making party, open house, and Christmas Day celebration.

Cookie exchange

The purpose of the cookie exchange—besides having fun with friends—is to go home with a great variety of cookies for holiday eating while only having to bake one kind yourself. The cookie exchange requires each participant to bake enough cookies to share. After the total attendance count is known, the hostess calls each guest and tells her how many dozens of cookies she will need to bring—typically one dozen for each of the other guests.

At one cookie exchange I attended, I had to bring each dozen cookies on a separate paper plate and I went home with several plates of cookies. My daughter went to an exchange last year and was simply required to bring eight dozen cookies in one container. She returned home with the same container filled with a mix of the other girls' cookies. The girls played games and watched a Christmas video while an adult divided up all the cookies. Hot cocoa, popcorn, and (what else!) cookies were served.

201 Caroling

One of my fondest childhood memories is going Christmas caroling in Yuma, Arizona, with people from the church that my father pastored. Before leaving, we changed from our shorts into jeans and sweaters, since the evening temperature was usually in the fifties. A few carloads of enthusiastic singers descended on some unsuspecting street and went singing door to door.

In the iciness of a Colorado Springs December evening, the kids from our church prefer to sing to the residents of retirement or convalescent homes. The evening ends with hot cocoa and goodies at someone's home. It is a good reminder to our healthy youngsters that there are people we rarely see who are lonely and hurting.

202 Christmas craft party

My sister and her husband host a Christmas craft party in their home every year. Sue and

Jerry invite friends from church, work, and the neighborhood, along with nearby family members, to make gingerbread houses and tree ornaments. While Sue provides the beverages, the guests bring plates of snacks to share. Sue carefully thinks through the crafts and provides all the materials. She has a couple of hot glue gun stations placed where people will not trip over the cords. Food is served in the kitchen. With carols playing in the background, new friendships are formed, old friends are reunited, and crafts are made. My sister's large home can accommodate the large crowd working at several tables.

My daughter and I plan to host a gingerbread house party this year. The houses will be constructed using graham crackers, white icing, and a variety of candies. We will invite a lot fewer people than my sister would. Anna and I think we can squeeze about a dozen people around two work tables.

203 Open house

The most efficient way to have a lot of people over for a Christmas party is to host an open house. Your guests can drop by anytime during the designated hours so you probably will not have all of them there at once. Most people like to circulate and talk with other guests.

The biggest concern for the hostess is providing enough food and beverages. You will need to enlist help to ensure all the food trays, ice buckets, and beverages are constantly replenished. Assign someone else to occasionally walk around picking up trash and deserted drinks. People can consume a lot while standing around visiting, so plan on several servings of finger foods per person.

Serve a variety of foods, such as cookies, fudge, cheese cubes, Swedish meatballs, fresh fruit, deviled eggs, and vegetable sticks with dip. Besides the usual coffee or punch, provide a pitcher of water and soft drinks.

As with the Super Bowl party discussed in chapter 5, there are three ways to prepare all that finger food. The most expensive but easiest way is to order trays of food from the grocery store deli or have the food catered. A slightly cheaper alternative is to see what is available in the freezer section of your local price club. Tiny quiches, meatballs, dips, Mexican taquitos, minipizzas, and (my personal favorite) cream puffs are often available. The alternative that requires the most work is preparing all the food yourself. If you choose this alternative, begin a few weeks ahead of time, freezing what you can. Enlist a few girlfriends to help you in the kitchen the day before the party.

The easiest alternative, of course, is to have all comers bring a plate of goodies to share. Personally, this last choice is not my favorite because I like to give my open-house guests a break from food preparation. I want to *bless* them!

204 Christmas Day celebration

One of our Christmas traditions is to invite people over who have nowhere else to go on Christmas Day. Our circle of friends—families and singles—includes some who cannot make it across this big country to be with their closest relatives, so we adopt them for the day.

Reality Check

Gorgeous decorations, a perfect feast, and lovely presents are not what make Christmas magical and meaningful. Too many commitments and trying to get your home to match the ones in magazines will only add stress and take your attention away from what is really important.

You'll find more meaning in your holiday by spending time with those you care about and remembering it is the birth of our Savior that we are celebrating. Many of my friends have decided to forgo the craziness of preparing a Christmas Day feast by spending the day as a family serving the less fortunate at our local homeless mission. They report feeling very blessed.

According to our friends it means a lot to celebrate Christmas in a home with a bunch of loving people. They share in the glow of family camaraderie. I invite them to bring one of their family's traditional dishes to round out our feast. They have treated us to some yummy traditions!

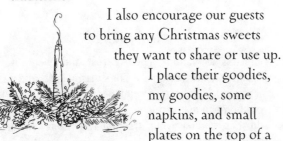

I also encourage our guests to bring any Christmas sweets they want to share or use up. I place their goodies, my goodies, some napkins, and small plates on the top of a card table that is set up in a corner of the living room. For beverages, I serve a Crock-Pot of spiced apple cider that I start after breakfast so everyone can enjoy it all day. My collection of Christmas mugs is set out next to the Crock-Pot. Since no two mugs are alike, it is easy for guests to remember which one is theirs.

Festive table decorations for Christmas

As you prepare to decorate for any of these Christmas festivities, you may find that you do not have to buy anything. Look at what you own with an imaginative eye.

205 Add tiny sprigs of evergreen to a bowl or basket filled with shiny ornaments.

206 Decorate candles with festive ribbons.

207 Spread greenery with pine cones and holly berries on a tray or table runner.

208 Add a big festive bow to a basket of pine cones and sprigs of greenery.

209 Wrap an array of empty boxes so that they look like festively-wrapped presents.

210 Decorate tiny evergreen trees—real or artificial—with miniature decorations.

211 Weave a garland around candlesticks.

212 Add Christmas picks to a houseplant.

213 Arrange a collection of angels, Santas, snow globes, or other Christmas collections on a tray or table runner.

214 Arrange holly and evergreens in a vase.

215 Brighten any room with poinsettias. (Sadly, killing these plants is another one of my traditions.)

216 **Quick and thrifty gift ideas**

Have you ever needed to give a lot of gifts to a number of people who would all be there to see what the others received? You need to give something that everyone will appreciate and that won't kill your budget. Or perhaps you want to reach out to neighbors or acquaintances from the garden club. Now it is time to get resourceful.

Homemade gifts are often easiest on the budget, and with fancy presentation they can appear rather impressive. Ribbons, bows, raffia, pretty tissue paper, or squares of fabric and tulle are inexpensive. Get creative with whatever you have on hand. Quality gift stores present their merchandise stylishly—pick up ideas from them.

First, of course, you'll want to decide what you will be making. See the bibliography at the end of this book for ideas on where to find detailed instructions. Some great ideas for Christmas gifts include:

- Candy
- Fudge
- Large, gourmet-style cookies
- Jams and jellies
- Homemade cookie mixes, soup mixes, or brownie mixes in mason jars
- Potpourri
- Fruit and nut baskets
- Bath salts
- Stationery made by stamping on good-quality paper
- Birdhouses you build and paint to suit each family's style or colors

- Service certificates that fit your talents (scrapbooking, photography, computer help, gardening, housecleaning, car maintenance)
- Framed calligraphy
- Framed family portrait

What if you are short on time? What can you purchase that doesn't cost too much but that everyone will appreciate receiving? Any of the items mentioned above or:

- Gift certificates to a store or restaurant (Our circle of friends has responded well to certificates to bookstores and coffee-houses. What do you and your loved ones have in common?)
- A short book that means something to you
- Gourmet teas or coffees
- Kitchen linens
- Candles

217 Christmas traditions

Traditions are those special activities you and your family do year after year. Your kids or grandkids can rely on them happening, giving them a sense of security. You probably have some and do not even realize it. They could be:

- Special decorations, music, or food
- The recipes you prepare each Christmas
- The time when your family open gifts
- A Christmas Eve service
- The same silly jokes
- Or even what Dad wears on Christmas Day every year

One of my personal traditions seems to be that I commit some really horrible blunders when preparing the Christmas dinner. I've done everything from leaving the bag of giblets in the turkey to burning the croissants to forget-ting to serve a salad that was "hiding" in the refrigerator. The stories are legendary and grow more hilarious with each passing year. You know the interesting part? My friends and family like me a lot more (and expect a lot less from me) when they see firsthand that I am not perfect and can laugh over my mistakes with them.

218 New Year's Eve home celebration

When our children were young we liked to host a New Year's Eve celebration for a few close friends for one very selfish reason—we would not have to hire a baby-sitter if the party was at our house!

When we lived in Gresham, Oregon, we always invited over the same two couples and their children. They were our closest friends and our children were all compatible. We spent the evening eating the goodies we had all shared in preparing, and playing games. Eventually the kids were bedded down for the night, and the adults kept partying until the New Year arrived. At 12:01 we sang "Happy Birthday" to our friend with a January 1 birthday and had a birthday party with cake, candles, and gifts. A couple of the older kids emerged from one of the bedrooms claiming they could not get to sleep. After a piece of cake they seemed amenable to returning to bed.

Even though we are past the frustrating years of finding a baby-sitter for New Year's Eve, we continue to host a party that night. (The exception was the year we were invited to a black-tie affair. We had to forage for the correct formal wear, find a baby-sitter, and travel across town. It was fun to get all dressed up but we didn't have nearly as much fun as we normally do at our more relaxed home parties. Wearing high heels, holding my stomach in for hours, and making small talk

with mere acquaintances just are not my
personal ideas of fun.)

Whether you put on a black-tie affair or
humbly entertain a few old or new friends,
there is no place like home for this holiday.
We usually spend the evening playing cards
and board games while munching on finger
foods and sipping caffeine-free beverages. I like
bringing out the champagne flutes and filling
them with sparkling apple cider or grape juice
to toast the new year. The kids like to make
noise using wooden spoons on pot lids. At
exactly midnight we all go outside and watch
the fireworks that are lit on the top of Pike's
Peak. And so ends one year and begins another
for the Janssen Five and our friends.

"Over the river and through the wood—
Now Grandmother's cap I spy!
Hurrah for fun! Is the pudding done?
Hurrah for the pumpkin pie!"

—FROM "THANKSGIVING DAY," A POEM BY LYDIA MARIA CHILD

Chapter 12
Other Holidays

Last May I finally got tired of the pain in my left foot and had foot surgery. My family was pretty confident that they could run the household without me for a few weeks. To prove it, my husband decided to continue our tradition of having a few friends over for a Memorial Day cookout. Al invited a family of four and a couple of other friends.

While I listened from the sofa where I was keeping my toes above my nose, Anna and Al cleaned the house, decided on the menu, and prepared all the food after doing all the shopping. It was a simple, tried and true menu that began with soft drinks and chips and dips. Hamburgers and hot dogs were cooked on the grill and offered with buns, lettuce, tomatoes, onions, cheese, and the usual condiments. Al put together his favorite recipe of baked beans and sliced up a chilled watermelon. He had asked the guests to each bring a salad but didn't tell them what kind, so we enjoyed two tasty fruit salads. Blueberry and cherry pies were ordered from a nearby bakery and served with vanilla ice cream and freshly brewed coffee.

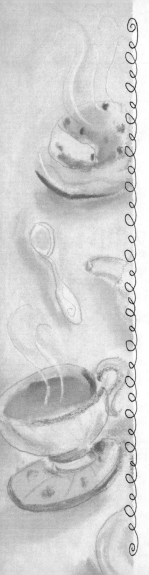

The gorgeous Colorado weather made it possible for the meal to be served buffet-style outside. Anna entertained the two visiting toddlers with outdoor activities so their parents could sit back and get a break from the constant supervision that little ones require. The atmosphere was relaxed as we sat around and visited. Since I could not do much, everyone was eager to help out. The best part of the evening was that I was able to be with friends while convalescing. It really helped ease the severe case of cabin fever I had been developing.

Our simple Memorial Day dinner is just one example of how easy it is to use holidays as an excuse for hospitality. Somehow those special days seem to have more meaning when we share them with others. It is another opportunity to bless people, catch up with old friends, and kickstart new friendships. Our menus are usually simple, but I try to make events more fun with a few appropriate festive touches.

VALENTINE'S DAY

Al and I are a bit rebellious about Hallmark directing our love life, so we have chosen to make Valentine's Day a fun time. Several traditions have developed over the years, and all are meant to tell our friends and family that we love them in silly, creative, and thoughtful ways. For minimal expense and just a little forethought we can spread a lot of love.

219 Guests

This is a ready-made opportunity to bless a couple who could use a night out without their little ones. Simply invite their children over for dinner. Better yet, have lots of kids over for a Valentine's Day party and strengthen many marriages!

As an alternative, invite your single

friends over for a meal. It can be a very lonely time, since there is social pressure to have a date on Valentine's Day. I am sure that dinner with friends expressing Christian love would be better than anything they had planned alone at home that evening.

Menu

220 Get carried away with pink and red colors and heart shapes when planning the menus for the day. If something is already pink or red, I serve it. Food coloring makes beverages, pancakes, scones, sugar cookies, and such the desired color.

221 Cookie cutters produce heart-shaped sandwiches, biscuits, and scones. Bake a coffee cake or a casserole in a heart-shaped baking pan. I often attempt, with mixed success, to create heart-shaped pancakes. My family is usually quite amused as the flapjacks often assume other unintended forms. (At such times deciphering the shape is a bit like cloud gazing.)

222 Our favorite Valentine's Day dinner is individual heart-shaped pizzas. I make the crusts and sauce and provide a variety of toppings so everyone can assemble their own custom pizza. I also toss a green salad with red onions, red cabbage, tomatoes, and radishes. Dessert is heart-shaped sugar cookies with pink or red icing, or colored sugar. Raspberry sherbet works when I do not have time to bake.

Centerpieces and decorations

Since nothing even remotely resembling a dozen red roses has arrived at my home in February, I make my own

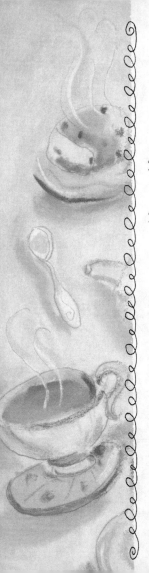

centerpiece and decorations. I usually transform what I am already using by adding a few touches to the dinner table.

223 Tie a red or pink ribbon or bow around a clay pot of flowers or a houseplant.

224 Make floral picks. At the end of a long stiff wire, I attach hearts made of felt, fabric, or construction paper and then insert the picks into a houseplant.

225 Use a lace tablecloth or doily under the centerpiece.

226 Spread Valentine confetti on the center of the table.

227 Gather a collection of attractive red, white, and pink items. It may include cards, statuettes, doilies, framed photos, a small vase holding a single flower, candles, or books. I arrange them on a tray, plate, doily, or cake pedestal.

228 Add red, pink, or white tapers or votive candles to the centerpiece.

EASTER

Easter gives us another opportunity to reach out to both our brothers and sisters in Christ and those we would love to see join the family of God. Most people grew up with some family traditions around this holiday, even if they do not celebrate the resurrection of our Lord Jesus Christ.

229 Guests

As with other holidays, our family usually looks around to see if anyone needs a place to go for Easter dinner. Our friends the Westerlunds invite the entire newlywed Sunday school class to their home for a planned Easter potluck dinner. Many of these couples are miles away from family.

Consider inviting neighborhood kids to your home the day your family decorates Easter eggs. I make sure they wear old clothes that will not be harmed by a little dye, glue, or paint. Some years we just dye the eggs. Other years we get out all the craft supplies and decorate blown-out eggs. More ideas on that later.

230 Menu

Several years ago I purchased some egg-shaped Jell-O molds. These are great fun, although creating interesting layers of colors takes time and patience. I enjoy making green Jell-O eggs and serving them on a bed of lettuce or shredded red cabbage with our Easter ham dinner. (Of course, our menu is green eggs and ham!)

231 Centerpieces and decorations

A few years ago my daughter decorated the eggs to resemble all the people who were coming for Easter dinner. The eggs were used as place cards. Construction-paper "collars" made the eggs stand up. Everyone had fun trying to figure out which egg was supposed to be him or her. Grandma Janssen's egg had curly white hair on it, glasses made of bent wire, and lace on her collar. My husband, Al, was seated by the egg with the collar on which a white shirt collar and tie had been painted. The egg's mustache was quite comical.

232 Easter egg hunt

The annual postdinner Easter egg hunt has been a family tradition for years. Our guests really get into it! The neighborhood kids can't stay away (loud laughter is irresistible) so we invite them to join in. We hide plastic eggs all over our yard and the kids collect them in their own baskets. Sometimes we pair older kids with little ones to even the playing field.

Some people color-code the eggs for each age group. The four- and five-year-olds hunt for the yellow eggs; the six- and seven-year-olds

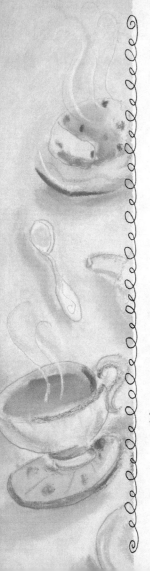

hunt for the blue ones; and so on. After all the eggs are discovered, the older kids like to hide the eggs again for the younger kids.

Once in a while, something unexpected happens. One year we discovered that an egg stuck in a car's tailpipe can be removed with a vacuum cleaner. Inevitably, we find a few stray eggs one or two months later while gardening.

Egg decorating

Invite your friends or your children's friends over for an afternoon of Easter egg decorating. The supplies are inexpensive; in fact, I usually just use whatever has accumulated in my craft cupboard. Be prepared for a mess, however.

233 Wooden eggs purchased at a craft store make long-lasting artwork.

234 Hard-boiled eggs have a limited life, so I usually have the kids decorate blown-out eggs—a tradi-tion that began when I was a kid. Beginning a couple weeks before Easter, blow out eggs as you use them. To do this, use the sharp point of a knife or similar object to poke a tiny hole in one end of the egg and also a larger (half-inch) open-ing on the other end. Over a bowl, blow on the small hole (wipe off your lipstick first!) and the egg will spurt out from the larger hole and into the bowl. Rinse out the eggshell and let it drain in an egg carton.

235 Eggs can be decorated intricately or simply. The artists may wish to sketch out the design on paper before sketching it with pencil onto the egg. Paints, paint pens, and markers work well. Beads, jewels, braids, ribbons, and sequins can be glued on.

236 Decoupage techniques can result in gorgeous eggs. Choose thin paper such as inexpensive gift-wrapping or printed tissue paper. Cut the paper into thin strips before carefully gluing

each onto the egg. Coat the finished egg with a few layers of decoupage glue.

237 Depending on which technique they use, the crafters may turn out animals, people, flowers, bugs, cartoon characters, stained-glass windows, buildings, or even Faberge-style creations. When lined up, they may resemble a family, zoo, garden, street scene, or jeweler's display.

238 Easter egg tree

Each year my mom displayed our priceless homemade art objects on an Easter egg tree. My mother would put a tree branch with many smaller branches in a pot of sand. We hung the eggs on the branches using bent paper clips. (My mom kept our blown-out egg creations. A few years ago she returned them all to her adult children. They brought back such memories!)

You can buy an Easter egg tree or make your own by bending stiff wire into a tree shape

and inserting it into a pretty pot filled with plaster of paris.

239 Easter egg carton

Several years ago my daughter came home from her Christian kindergarten with an egg carton full of a dozen numbered plastic eggs and a story to tell about each one. Each egg had a small item in it and an explanation of what the item represented. Together the dozen eggs told the story of Easter. This is a great way to tell young children the real significance of Easter.

Since Anna brought home her carton, I've seen this idea used in many other places, often with different contents in some of the eggs. However, if you want to make your own set, you might use the following:

Egg 1: A piece of a palm branch. People waved palm branches as Jesus rode on

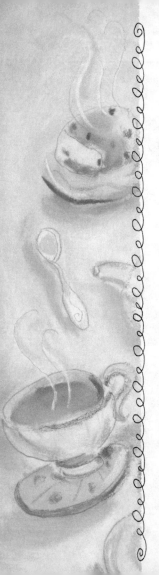

a donkey into Jerusalem (Matthew 21:7-11; Mark 11:7-11).

Egg 2: A tiny swatch of fabric scented with perfume. Mary poured valuable perfume on Jesus' feet (Matthew 26:6-13; Mark 14:3-9).

Egg 3: A piece of Chex cereal. Jesus and His disciples ate the Last Supper (Matthew 26:26-30; Mark 14:12-26).

Egg 4: Three small coins, real or fake. Judas betrayed Jesus for thirty pieces of silver (Matthew 26:14-25).

Egg 5: A cross. Jesus carried a cross to Golgotha (Mark 15:21-22).

Egg 6: Small piece of a thorny plant. Soldiers placed a thorny crown on Jesus' head (Matthew 27:29; Mark 15:17).

Egg 7: Swatch of plain fabric. Soldiers cast lots for Jesus' clothes (Matthew 27:35; Mark 15:24).

Egg 8: A nail. Jesus was crucified on the cross (John 19:16-18; Luke 23:33).

Egg 9: A chunk of sponge. The soldiers gave Jesus vinegar mixed with gall (a bitter acid) on a sponge to drink (Matthew 27:34; Mark 15:36).

Egg 10: A few whole cloves. Jesus' body was prepared for burial with linens and spices (Matthew 27:59; Luke 23:50-56).

Egg 11: A stone. Jesus was buried in a cave with a rock covering the opening (Matthew 27:60; Mark 15:46).

Egg 12: A swatch of white fabric. Jesus left his linen grave cloths behind when he arose from the dead (Luke 24:9-12; John 20:3-8).

PATRIOTIC CELEBRATIONS

I like to keep things casual and simple at these times so I can enjoy my guests—and the summer weather!

240 Guests

Most people are off from work or school on Memorial Day, the Fourth of July, and Labor Day, so they're great holidays to invite friends over. We prefer to entertain outdoors, which generally requires less work. Whether you have a custom-designed multilevel deck or a patch of cement outside your back door, you can set up a table or two and enjoy the great outdoors.

If children are expected, I suggest that families arrive earlier than usual so we can have more time with them before they must go home and put the kids to bed. Since dinner may be an hour or two away, I like to serve chips, dips, and drinks to tide them over until mealtime. I also provide playthings such as balls, croquet, bubbles, or sidewalk chalk.

241 Block parties

If you've wanted to get to know your neighbors and never had the opportunity, block parties held around a patriotic holiday may be the answer. For many years we lived on a quiet street in Salem, Oregon. The seven families on our street had a tradition of meeting together every Fourth of July on the Carrolls' front yard and driveway to eat ice cream sundaes and watch fireworks. Marylou Carroll let each family know what toppings and ice cream to bring, and each family also brought their own lawn chairs and fireworks.

As soon as it was dark, a fireworks display set off at the nearby fairgrounds entertained us. Then we lit sparklers and other small fireworks. (Yes, they were legal there at the time, though Roger Carroll always kept a few buckets of water handy.) Another neighbor brought her radio so we could keep track of police calls, which was also entertaining.

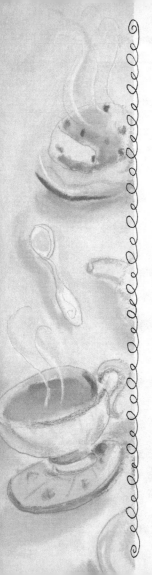

We miss those neighbors, who became like extended family to us!

With those Salem days in mind, a few years ago we organized a similar Fourth of July block party at our home in Colorado Springs. Since our driveway and front yard are the flattest on the street, we hosted the potluck. Everyone brought food, tables, chairs, and other supplies.

What's so great about a block party? For one thing, if a need comes up, someone is bound to have it at his or her house and it only takes a minute to get it. Also, no one is responsible for everything, so no one is overworked. The only extra cleaning I did before the Fourth of July party was to wipe down our downstairs bathroom and put out extra toilet paper.

242 Menu

Over the years we have pretty much perfected a simple patriotic holiday menu that we serve on our back deck. We eat hamburgers cooked on our old Weber grill. My family also expects a huge bowl of my potato salad. We eat watermelon the old-fashioned way, which includes a seed-spitting contest. Our patriotic dessert consists of cherry pie, blueberry pie, and vanilla ice cream.

Centerpieces and decorations

To make your table look especially festive, look around to see what could be adapted to create a patriotic grouping or centerpiece for your table.

∽∽∽∽ Reality Check ∽∽∽∽

Hamburgers always taste great when they're grilled; however, make them extra special for your guests by providing one or more of the following toppings:

- Avocado slices
- Mushrooms sauteed in butter
- Bacon
- Swiss or cheddar cheese
- Grilled onion rings

I use a set of solid white dishes, blue-checked napkins, and a red-checked tablecloth. A centerpiece pulls it all together. Some simple centerpiece ideas include:

243 Stuff a clay pot with floral foam, cover the foam with Spanish moss, and add small American flags.

244 Add small flags to a small houseplant or outdoor potted plant.

245 Display pots of red, white, and blue petunias or other flowers.

246 Toss patriotic confetti on the table.

247 Spread a few pictures or postcards of sites from Washington, D.C., Mt. Rushmore, the Statue of Liberty, or historical homes on your table.

248 Make a patriotic-looking bouquet of red, white, and blue balloons.

249 Stack a few history books, coffee-table books, or

biographies of famous Americans in the middle of the table and top with a small model of a significant American edifice such as the Statue of Liberty or the White House.

250 Arrange a collection of red, white, and blue candles on your table.

251 Display an apple pie and baseballs.

THANKSGIVING

Reaching out to those who have no family around is part of the Janssen Five Thanksgiving tradition.

252 Guests

Football is another family tradition—participating rather than just watching it on TV. About two hours before the feast, the guys like to work up an

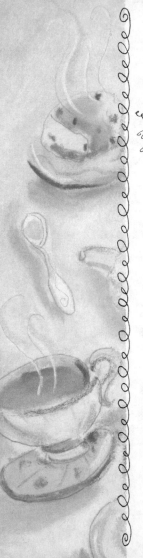

appetite playing a game of touch football at the park down the street. Each year we photograph the table with everyone seated just before we dig in to the meal. The feast, guests, and lovely decorations are recorded for posterity.

253 Menu

The Janssen Five expect the same menu with only minor alterations every year. It includes turkey, dressing, mashed potatoes, gravy, cranberry sauce, fruit salad, crescent rolls, and a variety of pies served with whipped topping. Most of the variation comes from our guests, who are invited to bring a dish that they consider part of their tradition.

254 Activities

In addition to touch football, Thanksgiving dinner includes a time when we give thanks for our blessings throughout the year.

We read a psalm before saying grace. During dinner we share what we are especially thankful for. Sometimes I put three pieces of dried corn on each plate to remind us of the hardship of the original pilgrims. Three pieces of corn was their daily allotment that first hard winter. Most did not survive.

Centerpieces

On Thanksgiving we set the table with our best linens and china. When the Janssen kids were younger, our table decorations usually were their school projects. Interesting pilgrims and various types of turkeys graced our dining tables during those years.

More sophisticated centerpieces can be purchased at a florist or grocer. Silk arrangements will last for years. Other ideas include:

255 Grow your own gourds or fall-blooming flowers such as mums and asters. (Of course, this takes some planning ahead!)

256 Collect interesting dried flowers and seed pods from a field and use them to make an arrangement.

257 Gather fall leaves and spread them on the table. One year my kids helped me dip some in melted red wax so that they stayed pretty until it was time to decorate for Christmas. Add pinecones for a variety of color and texture. You might place a few candles in the middle.

258 Visit the library to find craft books for your children. They can fashion pilgrims, turkeys, log homes, and friendly Indians for your centerpiece.

259 Make candleholders from apples, pinecones, gourds, or small pumpkins. Use an apple corer to make a hole for the candle. You may need to slice a bit off the bottom of the produce to make it stand straight. Place the candleholders on a platter or something to protect your table linens.

260 Hollow out a large squash and use it as a flower arrangement container. It will not hold water for long, so insert a small jar or glass for that purpose.

261 Add fall floral picks to a houseplant or a potted mum.

"I really think you had better come and stop with me for a little time. It's very plain and rough, you know—not like Toad's house at all—but you haven't seen that yet—still, I can make you comfortable."

—Water Rat to Mole in *The Wind in the Willows* by Kenneth Grahame

Chapter 13
Overnight Guests

Soon after Al and I were married, an old friend called to say he would be in town for a few days. Al invited him to stay with us in our little apartment. It never occurred to Al that we did not have a guest room. It didn't bother our guest either. He was quite comfortable sleeping on our hand-me-down sofa.

Over the years we have accommodated many overnight guests in various ways. When our kids were younger, they sometimes gave up their bedrooms when families with young kids visited. The three slept in a tent in the backyard

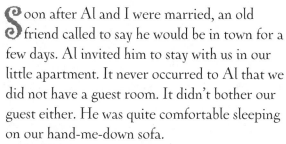

with their guests. For several years we kept a sofa bed in our home office so it could do double duty as the guest room. In our current home we have a guest room as well as a sofa bed in our family room. With all the extra beds and sofas, we can put up a family of six overnight.

Whether you are anticipating an old friend's quick, just-passing-through-town visit or Cousin Franny and her family of four who will be staying for a week, you can do a lot to make their stay more comfortable and to give yourself greater peace of mind. Like most

successful interpersonal interactions, you need to begin by talking.

IMPORTANCE OF COMMUNICATION

Some of our overnight guests have invited them-selves to stay with us and others have come at our invitation. Either way, I need precise infor-mation to make it a smooth visit for all of us.

First, I need to know their arrival and departure times. I cannot wait at home all day for someone who he thinks he'll arrive "sometime on Monday." If my guests are driving and cannot predict the exact time of their arrival, I ask that they call when they get within an hour or two of my home. Since nearly everyone owns a cell phone, there is little excuse for not calling ahead.

Likewise, I need to know the date and approximate time of my guests' departure so I can schedule around that and plan to do as much together as possible before they have to leave.

It's also helpful to discuss the following:

• Do your guests have any dietary restrictions?
• Are they coming for a special event? When is it? Will you be invited or expected to attend?
• Is there anything special they want to do or see in your area?
• Will they be contacting other friends in the area while they are in town? When?
• Will they be parking their vacation-home-on-wheels on your property? If so, will they need hookups?
• If children are coming, will they need special sleeping accommodations such as a crib or playpen? How about a high chair?
• Will they be bringing any pets?

Once your guests have arrived and had time to freshen up and unpack, sit down and have a frank discussion about expectations and schedules. The most important schedule may be the use of bathrooms. Will they be sharing the bathroom with your family? When will everyone be taking a shower? Does your company need to be sensitive to when family members need the bathroom at certain times to get ready for work and school?

Then there are meal and scheduling questions. Will your guests be there for every meal? Talk about your breakfast routines and when you customarily eat lunch and dinner. Factor in the schedule of activities during the duration of their visit and talk through a rough schedule for each day, when everyone will be coming and going. Let them know about any appointments and other commitments that you have they need to be aware of. Write it all on the calendar for quick reference.

I like to plan some private time in my schedule when guests are around. Too much togetherness gets old. Tactfully feel out whether your guests really want you along for everything they

do. If you already have commitments, that will provide a natural reason to go your separate ways for a few hours.

MI CASA ES SU CASA: MAKING GUESTS FEEL AT HOME

Getting everything out in the open is an important beginning to a pleasant time with friends; but there are many other ways to make your guests feel at home.

262 Welcoming houseguests

What says "welcome" to houseguests?

- An easy-to-read house number
- The front porch light on
- A clean front porch with a welcome mat
- Your smiling presence and kind words
- Help with luggage
- A clean, comfortable guest room and bathroom

- The offer of a cold drink of water
- The happy anticipation in your voice

263 Open your kitchen to guests

I like to make my entire home guest-friendly. First-time houseguests are invited into my kitchen, where I show them around. Since our breakfast routine is usually self-serve, I point out where everything is stored. I open the pantry doors to reveal the crackers, granola bars, cookies, nuts, and paper napkins that I keep together for snacks. Next I show them the beverage center. My mugs, coffee, tea, cappuccino, cocoa, and sugar bowl are stored next to the stove top where I keep a kettle. I show them how to operate our microwave to heat water for tea and where to find water glasses. I do all this because I want my houseguests to feel free to get themselves a drink or snack without feeling as though they are imposing on me. I want them to feel at home.

264 Make the laundry room available

Folks who've been on the road awhile often appreciate my offer to use my laundry room. For this reason, I try to catch up on my laundry before their arrival.

265 Provide amusements

I cannot entertain my houseguests 24/7. I would get exhausted and they would get tired of me. For that reason, I try to keep other amusements out and available.

Quite often our friends enjoy our extensive library. (That is what happens when two writers marry!) In the living room we keep current magazines, the newspaper, and coffee-table books. Some of my guests like to do crossword puzzles so I often purchase a new book of puzzles for them to use and then take home with them. They find pencils in mugs we have scattered all over our home—it's another writers' thing!

Kids often need more action. Our garage is full of just about every imaginable kind of sports equipment. The basketball hoop in our driveway probably gets used the most. We also keep sidewalk chalk, art supplies, books, games, and toys available.

266 Baby-proof your house

While I'm on the subject of very young houseguests, I should say more about getting your home ready for them. You and their parents will go crazy trying to protect both them and your belongings if you do not do some babyproofing. Even the best behaved little one may find your priceless vase too tempting, so you had better put it and other fragile valuables away. Insert plastic plugs in all electrical outlets. Put poisonous substances out of reach.

Tie up cords that dangle from your window treatments. Crawl around the entire house on your hands and knees to spot other potential dangers.

THE JANSSEN FIVE B & B

Al and I have stayed at a budget motel near the freeway. We have also luxuriated at our local five-star resort, the Broadmoor. You can guess which one we would love to revisit.

In the interest of creating as much Broadmoor ambiance as we can, we are attempting to furnish our guest room with as many luxuries as we can squeeze into a nine-foot-by-ten-foot room. It is a work in progress.

Reality Check

The true bare necessities for overnight guests are a comfortable place to sleep, some privacy, access to a bathroom, nutrition, and your generous hospitable attitude.

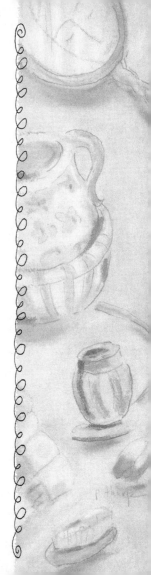

The Janssen B & B currently requires guests to share a bathroom with our daughter. Guests do have a room to themselves, albeit a small one. They sleep on a queen-sized bed, have a closet and dresser to themselves, and even get to walk on an old Persian rug. One side of the bed has a small table with a reading lamp. Since there isn't room on the other side of the bed for a table, I mounted a four-inch by twelve-inch shelf to the wall to keep miscellaneous items handy. On the back of the door I have installed three robe hooks and a full-length mirror. Another mirror hangs above the dresser. A night-light helps our guests move around at night. In true bed-and-breakfast fashion, the room is decorated with a bit of Victorian flair. Our guests love it.

THE PERFECT GUEST ROOM

Although you may not have a separate room for guest accommodations, you can still provide a comfortable private place for your guests.

Consider my description of the perfect guest room not as an unattainable dream but as a list of ideas that can inspire you to do the best you can for your guests.

267 The door to the guest room

To ensure your guest's sense of privacy and security, the guest-room door needs to be soundproof and lockable. Guests dislike it when friendly toddlers come barging in. They do appreciate their conversations or snoring remaining confidential.

The back of the door should have one or two robe hooks firmly attached. Spoil your guests by hanging luxurious white terry bathrobes on the hooks. Your guests will think they are visiting a five-star resort. More about the resort idea later.

268 The bed

Most couples prefer at least a queen-sized bed; however, two twin-sized beds give you more

flexibility. You can leave them separated when you house two choir members on tour or need to house a couple of kids. The beds can be pushed together when a married couple visits. The mattresses should be fairly firm and free of lumps, sags, and strange scents.

A dual-control electric blanket will solve most warmth issues. Otherwise, provide a couple of blankets or a down comforter. Keep extra blankets in the closet or folded neatly at the foot of the bed.

People are picky about pillows, so provide a variety. Many people sleep with two. On a bed for two people have at least two medium-density pillows and two low-density (soft) pillows. Some people are allergic to down and feathers so have alternatives handy.

If space allows, leave about two feet of free space on all sides of the bed for moving around. This also allows people to kneel by the bed for evening prayers.

Buy sheets with the highest thread count you can afford. Pure natural cotton is the most comfortable. In the winter, flannel sheets feel warmer.

269 The bedside table

On a table on at least one side of the bed provide the following:

- Reading lamp
- Box of facial tissues
- Electric blanket controls
- An electric alarm clock that is easy to read at night
- Water carafe and water glass
- Leave room for your guest's Bible and personal items

270 The closet

Leave plenty of space for your guests to hang their clothing. Provide padded hangers for

most of their garments, plus a few wooden suit hangers and skirt hangers. Keep the floor clear for shoes. Remember that your guest may need to store his luggage in the closet if there is not space elsewhere in the room. Install a small chest, microwave or TV cart, or a similar piece in a corner of the closet so your guests can stash their suitcases out of sight while still keeping them easily accessible.

271 The windows

For privacy and light control, nothing beats blackout curtains or drapes. Even those who prefer to have a devotional time at the crack of dawn may wish to sleep in now and then. If you ever took a sewing class, you have the skills needed to sew in light-blocking liners to your existing window treatments.

Step 1: Purchase enough of the light-blocking lining fabric to match the size of your existing curtains or drapes. You may have to sew lengths of the fabric together or do some trimming to achieve the correct size.

Step 2: Remove the curtains from the windows. Lay them on a clean, flat surface, outer side down. The inside of the curtains will be facing up.

Step 3: Lay the linings directly on the curtains. Make sure both curtains and liners are flat and smooth. Line up edges perfectly.

Step 4: Turn the edges of the lining fabric under just enough so that about a half-inch of the hem around the perimeter of the curtain is showing. Pin the lining in place carefully.

Step 5: Get some assistance in lifting the curtains to make sure they still drape well with the linings pinned in. If it looks good, proceed. If not, unpin and try again.

Step 6: Carefully sew the lining to the curtains by hand, using a whip stitch and being mindful to catch only the inside hem fabric of the curtain. If you catch fabric from the outer layer of curtain, the stitches will show.

Step 7: Rehang the curtains.

272 The other basics

Adding just a few more items to the room will make it quite suitable for houseguests.

- Night-light to help prevent bruised shins
- Chest of drawers with at least a few top drawers empty and lined
- Mirror
- Soft rug by the bed
- Cushy chair
- Alarm clock
- Bible

273 The luxuries

If you have the room and the budget, and you want to give your guests the ultimate five-star treatment, here are some luxuries you might include:

- Television and TV guide
- VCR or DVD player with an assortment of great flicks
- Radio
- Fresh flowers
- Easy chair next to a table and lamp
- Desk with quality stationery
- Bedroom slippers and white-terry bathrobe
- Well-stocked refrigerator
- Variety of reading material, such as devotional books, a Bible, some short story collections, and a magazine or two

A possible drawback to providing deluxe digs is that you may encounter delayed departure times!

274 A guest guide

Use a folder or three-ring binder to hold information for your out-of-town guests. You may want to include the following:

- A map of your area with your home highlighted for easy reference
- Pamphlets from places of interest in your area. You may want to highlight them on the map as well.
- Copies from a recent newspaper of the current schedules for local art shows, theater, concerts, movies, or other special events
- Maps to hiking trails, natural wonders, parks, and other outdoor attractions
- If you belong to AAA, include the tour book for your state.

- A local restaurant guide
- A piece of paper with your name, address, and phone number on it for them to take with them.
- A house key
- If you have a security code, include that too.
- A recent church bulletin listing service times. It will also give them a glimpse into the style of your worship service.

275 Naming the guest room

The Janssen Five may not be able to pull off the full five-star treatment, but we do honor our guests by naming our guest room after them. We try writing in calligraphy or using our computer to write in large, fancy lettering "The Ellis Room," or whatever the name of our incoming guests happens to be. We frame the paper, using glass, matting, and a handsome frame to complement our décor. The picture hangs next to the door to the guestroom at about eye level. Each time a new guest is due to arrive, we change the name of the room, swapping out the paper in our frame.

THE PERFECT GUEST BATHROOM

So the in-laws are on their way and you're pretty certain the guest bath won't pass their white-glove inspection. Follow this list and wash your worries away. First, consider this a good time to clean out the cupboards, medicine cabinets, and that scary mess under the sink. Clear off the countertops and reevaluate all the decorative items. If they look dated or hopelessly grungy, throw them out. (You just got a glimpse of Jo Ann, the Unrepentant Tosser, who is married, of course, to Al, the Unrepentant Keeper.) Sometimes it is better to have no decorations than to have tacky ones.

276 Cleaning the guest bathroom

The complete guide is rather intimidating. Realistically, I just do as little as I can get away with. But just in case you have the time, motivation, and energy, following my cleaning guide will result in the cleanest bathroom you have ever had. Now gather your cleaning supplies and start at the top and work your way down. (Or better yet, give this list to your teen and have him or her do it!)

- Wipe down the ceiling and walls, looking to eliminate fingerprints, water stains, hair, hair-spray residue, splashed cosmetics, and dust. If the ceiling fan needs cleaning, do it.
- Clean off the top of the shower curtain rod or shower-stall doors.
- Dust the top of the door frames, window frames, and medicine cabinets.
- Wash the shower curtain and bath mat.

- Remove water and mildew stains on the tub, shower, and wall tile.
- Replace any missing or worn grout and caulk.
- Use white vinegar to remove built-up water residue on shower doors or wall tiles.
- Make windows, mirrors, and glass shower doors shine.
- Wipe off any shelves, pictures, or other wall decorations.
- Use an old toothbrush to scrub around faucets and spigots, all crevices and seams.
- Wipe down everything that sits on the counters, shelves, and the top of the toilet tank.
- Clean the toilet, sink, and countertops.
- Wipe down doors on the vanity.
- Do not forget little details that might need shining like the toilet paper holder, towel racks, knobs on drawers and doors, light fixtures, or any visible plumbing.
- Clean the top edge of the floor trim.
- Mop the floor by hand. That old toothbrush efficiently cleans the seams, cracks, and crevices where two surfaces meet. While you're down there clean the floor trim as well.

Now the room sparkles! Bring on the white gloves.

277 A basket of emergency supplies

Guests sometimes forget toiletries or fail to anticipate their needs. Spare them the trouble and embarrassment of asking for something by providing the most commonly needed items for them. Besides the extra toilet paper, box of facial tissues, soap, and additional towels, fill an attractive basket or bowl with:

- New toothbrush (still in its package) and toothpaste

- Dental floss
- Disposable paper cups
- Pain relievers
- Emery board
- Nail clippers
- Small scissors
- Disposable shaver and shaving cream
- Lotion
- Hair spray
- Band-Aids
- Shampoo and conditioner (you can collect them when you stay at a hotel)
- Shower cap
- Comb
- Luxury items such as bath salts, bubble bath, and bath oils
- Feminine hygiene products if female guests are coming

278 The well-equipped guest bathroom

- Begin with a door that locks. Attach robe hooks on the back of it.
- Luxurious bath towels should be stacked or hanging. Show guests where extras may be found.
- The bath or shower should have a fresh bar of bath soap.
- The bath mat should be clean and ready.
- If your water controls are tricky, demonstrate how they work.
- Have extra rolls of toilet paper out or explain where they are kept.
- Facial tissues, paper cups, hand soap, and hand lotion should be clearly available.
- A night-light will assist guests during the night.

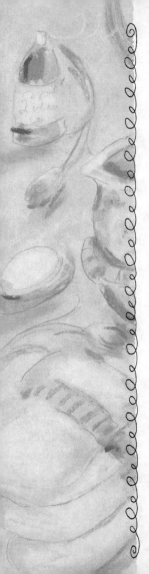

- Bathroom spray or a candle with matches next to it should be near the toilet.
- For extra luxury, have a hair dryer handy, hanging on the wall.
- I like to use decorative pump bottles for the liquid soap and hand lotion in my bathrooms. I buy both products in bulk and transfer the lotion and soap to the pretty pump bottles that match my décor. To avoid confusion, I use fingernail polish, which comes in just about every imaginable color, to write *Lotion* or *Soap* on the top of each container. A local craft store carries permanent ceramic paints that would probably work even better.

"And the prince took Marabelle to be his bride. *They lived happily ever after,* ruling over the land and encouraging all their people to love and serve God." (italics mine)

—*A Child's First Book of Virtues* by Emily Hunter

Chapter 14
Elly Revisited

The unstoppable Elly Parker has invited Pastor Schubert and his family over for dinner again. But this time, things will be different. It has been a year since her last attempt (okay, disaster), which prompted her to step back and take a good look at herself.

What she saw was a women who was overcommitted, stressed, way too self-centered, too conscious of what others thought of her, and sadly discontent. She also realized that serving an elaborate meal in a perfectly decorated home was never going to happen. Crystal and candlelight would probably never be her style. However, she was becoming very comfortable serving simpler family meals such as her five-alarm, award-winning chili.

Her motivations have changed. She no longer seeks to impress anyone with her hostessing expertise, her home, or her cooking abilities. Instead, she looks for opportunities to bring comfort, meet needs and, yes, bless other people. After much prayer and study, she realizes that her main spiritual gift is mercy. Her home is often the site for practicing that gift.

Her first attempt at hospitality had been clouded with self-doubt. She was sure that her usual dinner fare would not be acceptable. And what would the Schuberts think of having to eat off mismatched, well-worn, dated stoneware? Then there was her home. She knew for a fact that most of her fellow parishioners lived in much larger, lovelier homes. Hers seemed so old, cramped, and shabby in comparison. Practicing contentment had changed her opinion of her circumstances. Her home went from being an embarrassment to being a gift from God.

Elly's stewardship of that gift had changed, as well. Instituting a cleaning schedule resulted in a much more orderly home. She rarely completes the list every Thursday as planned but still the difference is remarkable. The kids are learning, with a great deal of supervision and encouragement, how to properly clean the house. They like bringing their friends into this new, neater environment.

The meager budget that she used to complain about now seems more than adequate. There always seems to be enough to give generously to those in need. This careful steward now follows a budget, plans her meals, and knows where every dollar goes. It may sound restrictive, but Elly finds that it is actually very freeing.

Elly's year has been one of growth. In response to the lessons God has been teaching her about contentment, stewardship, and exercising her spiritual gifts, she has been methodically honing her hospitality skills.

It began when her Bible study leader mentioned that they could not meet at the church the following week because the carpets were being cleaned. Elly's hand shot up as if it had a life of its own. Having eight women meet in her living room turned out to be less work than she had imagined. Her family helped her clean the house. After all the women left, Elly realized that this was a form of hospitality she could do easily and often.

Her next step was huge and unplanned. Not long after she hosted the Bible study, Paul's Aunt Bess and Uncle Tom called to tell them that they were going to be driving across the country and would like to stop for three days to visit them and see some tourist attractions.

Thankfully they gave her several weeks notice. She plotted out all that had to be done to entertain a middle-aged couple for three days. The first thing on the list was to prepare a guest room. It was currently the place where they put stuff that they didn't know what to do with, such as old clothes, broken toys, tax returns, and holiday decorations. It seemed that the whole house and all the closets had to be cleaned out to accommodate the guest room clutter. Several bags went to the Salvation Army thrift store. Eventually, the bed was cleared, the closet emptied, and a dresser drawer was freed up. The room was not decorated as nicely as Elly would have liked, but it was clean and comfortable. She resolved to never let it get messed up again. She *would* deal with stuff as it came up.

Next Elly started thinking about how to entertain them. She got many ideas from her city's Web site. The library had books about hiking and parks in the vicinity. She asked her Bible study friends how they entertained out-of-town guests, and they offered even more ideas. Elly made up a file folder full of information on places to go, things to see, and interesting activities.

Meanwhile she also considered what to feed these relatives.

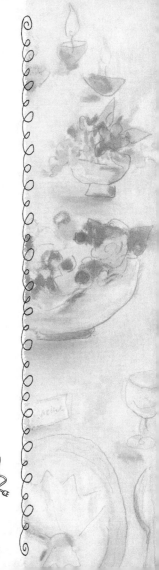

Elly's creativity froze. All confidence in her cooking abilities left her. The budget didn't allow fancy foods or a lot of eating out. Again she humbly sought the help of her friends. Again they came through for her. First they reminded her that the casseroles she brought to church potlucks were always the first to go. She was famous not only for her chili, but also for her Mexican chicken casserole and the lasagna made with Italian sausage.

Now that she had her dinners planned she wondered what to serve at breakfast and lunch. Her friends encouraged her to serve whatever she normally served for breakfast. Then they brainstormed lunch ideas. They discussed the foods they order when they eat out for lunch.

Reality Check

"Keep fervent in your love for one another. . . .
Be hospitable to one another without complaint."
(1 Peter 4:8-9, NASB).

Elly could make some of those. She had a good minestrone recipe she could make ahead. Cold-cut sandwiches served on good bread were easy. Dinner leftovers might even be acceptable one day. The menu monster was soon tamed.

The three-day visit went well. Her kids didn't embarrass Elly too much. They seemed to remember the manners Elly and Paul had been working on with them lately. The meals were all well-received—except the Mexican chicken casserole. Aunt Bess dislikes chicken. She graciously suggested that she would be happy with some of the leftover chili.

It turned out that Elly need not have worried about entertaining her company. They had done their own research and knew exactly what they wanted to do and see. They had come equipped with their own maps and directions as well. The first night they were there they all had a frank discussion about what they wanted to do alone and what activities they thought would be fun to do with everyone. Elly loved Aunt Bess and Uncle Tom! These seasoned travelers knew precisely how to be good guests. What a relief for Elly.

There were some glitches. The guests shared a bathroom with the two kids. Uncle Tom seemed to require it for a lengthy time just when the kids were getting ready for school. The kids ended up using their parents' bathroom and Elly found some extra tooth-brushes she had stored somewhere. Uncle Tom appeared oblivious to the problem and Elly was not sure how to mention the delicate matter so they just adjusted. (It would be their private joke later.) There were other snafus, but good humor, flexibility, and graciousness smoothed them over.

After Bess and Tom left, Elly and Paul discussed the visit over a cup of coffee. They agreed that their effort and even the inconveniences were worth it. The older couple was a wonderful example of marital commitment. They had told stories about Paul's ancestors that were new to him. They had also referred to the many times in their lives that God had answered their prayers and met their needs in miraculous ways. Aunt Bess had struggled to help her kids overcome their learning disabilities just as Elly was working to help her son overcome his. Elly and Paul felt that God had sent these people specifically to bless and encourage them just when and how they needed it.

Other hospitality opportunities presented themselves throughout the year. Before Elly would not have noticed them. Now she embraces them. Her confidence grew as she opened her home to singles at holidays, touring choir members, and various meetings. Each time she worried less and enjoyed it more. So finally, despite the missteps of the year before, as she waits for the Schuberts to arrive, Elly anticipates a lovely evening with the Schubert family.

Once again, the Schuberts are five minutes late. This time, however, they are greeted by a relaxed Paul and glowing Elly. The heavenly aromas of chili and cornbread draw them in. The home is neat and clean, the table is set, and dinner is ready. Who would believe that Elly spent most of the day with her family at the pumpkin patch?

Paul offers nonalcoholic pina coladas, which the adults and older children accept delightedly. The toddlers are given sipper cups of juice. After a few minutes of small talk, Elly invites Sue to help her put the finishing touches on a salad in the kitchen.

The ladies chat and laugh while tossing and dressing the salad and getting everything on the table. The Schubert toddlers want to help so they are given the baskets of cornbread to put on the table.

When Elly filled the Crock-Pot with chili that morning, she put out the fire in her five-alarm chili by omitting all the hot spices so that all the little ones would eat it. She now passes around a small bowl of chili powder for those who want to turn up the heat. The meal is relaxed and enjoyable, the tone set by Elly and Paul.

Not even a little disaster can ruin the ambiance this evening! When the youngest Schubert knocks over his bowl of chili, Elly and Sue calmly wipe up the table, floor, and child while sharing stories of other, worse disasters they have survived with their kids. Elly offers her homemade proverb: "Children are given to us to keep us humble." The kids don't get it.

After the leisurely dinner, the adults clear the table for a game of Rook. The older kids take the younger kids to the family room for quiet games and videos. Unlike that evening a year ago, the Schuberts are not at all anxious to flee to their home. Bedtimes are ignored since everyone is having such a great time!

The Schuberts eventually, reluctantly pack up the kids and move toward the front door. They mention their desire to have dinner again soon. Hugs and good-byes are exchanged before the door closes on a wonderful evening.

Paul warmly embraces his wife to congratulate her on a perfect evening. Funny, isn't it, that a year ago, Elly had frantically fussed attempting to fix a perfect feast that turned out to be a miserable failure. This time she worked within her comfort zone, and as a result, the Schuberts had left refreshed. Elly is tired but happy.

No longer interested in trying to put on the perfect dinner party, Elly effortlessly put on the perfect dinner party. Amazing! And now that you have read this book, you can do it too.

Event Planning Timeline for Dinner Parties and Large Events

Whether you are hosting an intimate dinner party or the entire adult Sunday school social, these guidelines and lists will help ensure that you cover all the details. The first section can be filled in four to eight weeks before an event, or as soon as you know you are hosting an event. Recording the major details at the outset will help keep you organized.

The rest of this appendix is organized by time: details you should handle four, three, and two weeks ahead, as well as one week, two days, and one day ahead. It even explains what to do the day of the event and the day after.

Under each heading are two lists. The first applies to any kind of meal with any number of people. The second list relates specifically to events with a large crowd of people. Keep in mind that not everything listed will be needed

for every get-together. For example, I rarely use place cards at dinner parties and only occasionally have a theme. Likewise, you may wish to add details unique to a party you are planning. Feel free to copy and reuse this guide.

Event Details

Date ....

Time ....

Reason for dinner (if any)....................................

Number of adult guests.......................................

Number of children...

Guest list and phone numbers ....

....

....

....

....

Theme...

Budget...

Menu ....

Special entertainment ....

Centerpiece and other decorations ....

....

Place cards..

Party favors...

Accommodations for seating, feeding, and entertaining young children ....

....

....

....

If no children will be present, what will I do with my children during the dinner party? ....

....

Four Weeks before Dinner:

- ○ Invite guests; provide maps with invitations
- ○ Put event on your master calendar/ personal planning device
- ○ Add guests and event to prayer list
- ○ Begin making lists:
  - ○ RSVPs
  - ○ Grocery lists for a week or two ahead and one for the day before party
  - ○ Shopping lists for other items such as place cards, centerpieces, decorations, favors
  - ○ Housecleaning schedule for week before party
- ○ Begin training your children in proper dinner etiquette
- ○ Place a pad of paper and pen on your bed-side table for those ideas you get when you are trying to sleep

For large crowd

- ○ Coordinate with committees
- ○ Finalize food plans
  - ○ Menu
  - ○ Who will supply it
  - ○ What you will do personally
  - ○ How it will be served (buffet or sit-down)
- ○ Arrange to rent, buy, or borrow:
  - ○ Chairs
  - ○ Tables
  - ○ Linens
  - ○ China
  - ○ Drinking glasses, coffee cups
  - ○ Flatware
  - ○ Tents
  - ○ Keep supplier's name, contact person, phone number, price, and availability for each of the above in one place
- ○ Name tags
  - ○ Who will make them?

○ How will they be distributed to guests?

○ Line up assistants for:

   ○ Setup ....

   ....

   ○ Greeters, name tags ....

   ....

   ○ Photography ....

   ○ Beverage server ....

   ○ Food server ....

   ○ Bathroom monitors ....

   ○ Cleanup crew ....

   ....

   ○ Other ....

   ....

   ....

○ Outdoor plans

   ○ Make backup plan for outdoor party

   ○ If overflow to backyard is possible, arrange to clean and set up outside chairs and tables

○ Decide whether to use signs or balloons to help identify home; if signs, assign their construction

Three Weeks before Party

○ Plan schedule for day before dinner party and day of party—include cleaning, cooking, and children's schedules. Expect to tweak this schedule up to the last minute.

○ Assemble centerpiece and other decorations that do not include fresh flowers or produce

○ Make arrangements for child care if needed

○ Decide what you will wear and make sure it is cleaned, mended, and fits

○ Decide which table linens you will use and iron them, storing them so they will not get wrinkled

○ Test new recipes

For large crowd

- ○ Stay in contact with committee members regarding party details
- ○ Begin to keep guest count
- ○ Plan seating of diners
- ○ Keep planning, shopping, and assistant lists current

Two Weeks before Party

- ○ Call any guests who have not responded
- ○ Finalize grocery lists
- ○ Buy nonperishables (such as trash bags, toilet paper)
- ○ Prepare and freeze any menu items you can
- ○ Make place cards
- ○ Purchase party favors
- ○ Make sure house address is well-lit and clearly visible from street

- ○ Research history and recent accomplishments of your guest of honor
- ○ Keep event and guests in prayer

For large crowd

- ○ Confirm availability and reservations of rented items
- ○ Figure out where to store guests' coats
- ○ Plan how you will serve foods; carefully think through logistics of buffet lines
- ○ Plan for ice buckets or tubs of ice for keeping drinks cold

One Week before Party

- ○ Confirm guest list
- ○ Review other lists to be sure everything is covered
- ○ Do special housecleaning; for example, the oven, chandelier, carpets

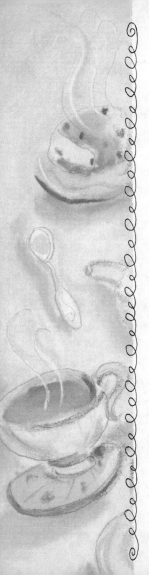

○ Polish silver; make sure china and serving pieces are clean

○ Fill salt and pepper shakers

○ Fold and set away napkins if doing fancy fold

○ Confirm child care

○ Continue to precook and freeze what you can

○ Inform neighbors if you will need spaces in front of their homes for guest parking

○ Keep praying

○ Refine schedule for party day, making sure it covers:

  ○ Cleaning

  ○ Emptying trash cans

  ○ Emptying dishwasher

  ○ Wiping down bathrooms

  ○ Final picking up and cleaning of public rooms

  ○ Food preparation schedule

○ Children's schedules

○ Time to get yourself and family dressed and ready

For large crowd

○ Figure out parking logistics; discuss with neighbors

○ Pick up items you are borrowing from friends

○ Talk to committee members about last-minute expectations

○ Confirm assistants

○ Begin to deep-clean public areas

○ If shoes will be removed at front door, prepare a sign or advise the greeter to cheerfully remind guests. Make room for all those pairs of shoes.

Two Days before Party

○ Clean house while praying for event

○ Clean out refrigerator to make room for dinner groceries

○ Buy fresh food and flowers

○ Arrange fresh flowers

○ Chill beverages

○ Begin to decorate

○ Clean out coat closet if you'll need it

○ Sweep walkway to front porch

○ Tidy up front yard; mow lawn

For large crowd

○ Remove furniture, art, and delicate objects to make room for crowds

One Day before Party

○ Make sure centerpieces, place cards, and favors are ready

○ Set table if possible

○ Put frozen foods in refrigerator to thaw

○ Buy or make ice

○ Launder kitchen linens

○ Keep praying for the event

○ Get a good night's sleep

For large crowd

○ Collect all borrowed/rented items

○ Set up tables and chairs

On Day of Party

○ Begin day with good breakfast and quiet time

○ Follow the schedule you've made for this day

○ Smile, go with the flow, have fun, keep your sense of humor

For large crowd

○ Designate someone to remain home all day to field phone calls, receive committee members helping with setup, and take deliveries

○ Put up signs or balloons identifying your home as the party location

○ Briefly review instructions with assistants as they arrive

○ Set up a place just inside the door for guests to get or write name tags

○ Put baskets full of toilet paper in each bathroom

○ Get yourself ready before the first person (usually an organizer who comes to check on things) arrives

Day after Party

○ Thank God for what he did the day before

○ Get organized with a hospitality notebook so you will not have to start from scratch each time. Include categories such as:
  ○ Date and reason for event
  ○ Guest lists—who you invited, food allergies, etc.
  ○ Menus and recipes
  ○ Resources
  ○ Ideas for future events
  ○ What you learned from this event that might apply to others

○ Serve leftovers for dinner

For large crowd

○ Write thank-you notes and include them when returning borrowed items

○ Return rented items

○ Keep records of where you got the best deals on rentals and other resources

A Food-to-People Ratio Guide

(or How Much Turkey Should I Buy for This Crowd?)

Most products have serving sizes listed on the package. But for those that do not, use my handy-dandy crowd-size serving guide. If you expect more people, do the math. I always like to cook a little more than the minimum required so I do not have to worry about exact serving sizes, big eaters (I almost said teenaged boys), and unexpected additional guests. Leftovers look terrific the next day when I'm too tired to cook.

FOOD	SINGLE SERVING SIZE	BUYING FOR 10 PEOPLE	REALITY CHECK
Beverages			
Punch	4 oz.	40 oz. or 5 cups	For 2–3 servings per guests, you'll need about one gallon
Coffee/tea	8 oz.	10 cups	Mugs hold more; guests generally drink more than one cup
Cream for coffee/tea	1 tablespoon	⅔ cup	Keep cream refill handy
Sugar	1 teaspoon	¼ cup	Fill the sugar bowl
Sugar substitute	1 packet	10 packets	Fill a pretty container
Desserts			
Sheet cake	2 ½-inch square	Half a store size; about 8-inch x 10-inch	For bigger pieces, buy more cake
Pie	⅙ of 9-inch pie	2 pies	If there is a variety of pies, some guests will want a sliver of each
Ice cream	½ cup	½ gallon	Who eats just ½ cup?
Dessert casseroles	3-inch square	9-inch x 12-inch	Precut to control serving sizes
Meat			
Meats with no bones	3–4 ounces	2 ½ pounds	Buy more for leftovers or seconds; preslice to control serving sizes
Ham with bone	½ pound	5 pounds	Order spiral-cut or preslice it yourself
Beef ribs	¾–1 pound	8–10 pounds	
Pot roast	½–¾ pound	6–8 pounds	Two 3–4 pound pot roasts
Whole fish	1 pound	10 pounds	One fish per person

FOOD	SINGLE SERVING SIZE	BUYING FOR 10 PEOPLE	REALITY CHECK
Meat (Continued)			
Fish steaks	1/3–1/2 pound	4–5 pounds	Precut servings
Cornish game hens	1/2 hen	5 hens	My son can eat a whole one
Whole chickens	1/4 bird	3 chickens	Serving equals one-half breast or drumstick with thigh
Chicken breast	1/2 breast	5 whole breasts	I like frozen, skinless, boneless, half breasts
Turkey under 12 pounds	3/4–1 pound	10 pounds	Easier to slice up 10 neat servings from larger turkey
Turkey 12 pounds and up	1/2–3/4 pounds		More meat per pound
Boneless turkey roast	1/3 pound	4–5 pounds	Plan for leftovers
Side dishes			
Soups/stews	1 cup	2 1/2 quarts	Cook at least 3 quarts
Tossed green salad	3/4 cup	2 quarts	Fill a big bowl
Potato salad or coleslaw	1/2 cup	5 cups	Prepare 1 1/2 quarts
Rice	1/2 cup cooked	1 2/3 cups raw rice or 2 1/2 cups instant	Make a little more, i.e. 2 cups raw or 3 cups instant
Vegetables	1/3–2/3 cups	Three 16 oz. cans or 2 pounds fresh/frozen	Check your recipe for more precise amounts
Butter/margarine	1/2 tablespoon	One stick, 1/4 pound	Plan on one stick or 8 oz. tub for every 8 guests
French bread	3/4-inch slice	1 loaf	An 18-inch loaf equals twenty-four 3/4-inch slices, including ends

Appendix C
Event Planning Timeline for Children's Birthday Parties

Planning a children's birthday party can be less stressful—even fun!—when you follow this timeline. Begin planning a children's birthday party by recording the main details first and then working through your to-do lists. In this appendix, those details are divided by the time when each detail should be completed.

Birthday Party Details

Name of birthday child...

Date of party..

Time of party...

Location (if not at home)...

Number of guests..

Theme...

Budget...

Menu ....

....

Party favor/gift bag contents.......................

....

Decorations...

Games/crafts/other activities............................

....

....

Guest list and phone numbers ....

....

....

....

....

....

....

....

Four Weeks before Party

O Make or buy invitations

O Put a list of guests and their phone numbers by the phone. Write "yes" or "no" next to each name as you receive RSVPs.

O Send invitations

O Put the party on your prayer list

O Plot party schedule—opening activity, games, food, opening of gifts, closing activity, etc.

O Reserve party place if not in your home

O Line up assistants to help lead games, monitor crowd, take photos

O Make shopping lists for:
    O Food
    O Goodie bags and contents
    O Materials for games, crafts, and other activities
    O Film
    O Birthday present and card

○ Balloons, candles, other decorations

○ Plates, cups, napkins, forks

Three Weeks before Party

○ Practice making any craft with your child to ensure it will work and to determine whether you'll need to borrow additional supplies (hot glue guns, scissors, etc.)

○ Order cake if you're not making it yourself

Two Weeks before Party

○ Make decorations

○ Buy goodie bags and contents

○ Gather game items

○ Arrange to borrow any other items needed

One Week before Party

○ Call those who did not RSVP

○ Assemble goodie bags

○ Purchase food, paper goods, other things on shopping lists

○ Buy, wrap, and hide gift and card for birthday child

○ Make and freeze ahead anything you can

○ Verify reservations if party will be held at outside location

○ Confirm assistants

○ Plan schedule for party day, including all meals, food preparations, appointments, craft and game preparations

Two Days before Party

○ Clean house

○ Begin to decorate

○ Clear out party space of extra furniture, valuable and fragile items, and rugs

○ Defrost frozen party food

○ Pick up items, such as chairs, tables, craft materials, that you're borrowing

○ Chill drinks

One Day before Party

○ Finish decorating

○ Bake cake if you are making it

○ Prepare any foods you can ahead of time

○ Make or buy ice

○ Prepare dinner ingredients to put into Crock-Pot next morning

On Day of Party

○ Follow schedule you previously made for this day or follow mine:

　　○ Start Crock-Pot dinner

　　○ Finish decorating home and clearing out party space

　　○ Pick up bakery cake

　　○ Set up crafts and games

○ Place your gift where other gifts will be collected

○ Do quick pickup of party areas

○ Get bathroom ready—quick wipe-down, set out clean towels and extra toilet paper

○ Put camera and goodie bags where you will not forget them

○ Set table

○ Get yourself and children cleaned and dressed

○ Close the doors to rooms that are not for public viewing

○ Be ready thirty minutes early

○ Coach assistants as they arrive

○ Begin an activity for kids to join when they arrive

○ Smile and enjoy the party

○ End the party at the designated time, having the kids ready to go and playing a quiet game or watching a quiet video when parents arrive. Make sure the birthday child sees each friend to the door, thanking him or her for coming and for the gift.

Day after Party

O Clean the house

O Put items back where they belong

O If you used a digital camera, print out photos with thank-you notes

O If you used a conventional camera, get prints made right away so you can include a snap-shot of each guest with the birthday child in each thank-you note

O Have birthday person write thank-you notes for gifts

O Write thank-you notes to assistants

O Return borrowed items with a thank-you note

O Return rented items

O Add helpful information to your hospitality notebook if you have one

Appendix D

Event Planning Timeline for Bridal and Baby Showers

Whether you're planning a wedding or baby shower, the details are nearly the same. Begin by recording the main details first and then working through your to-do lists. In this appendix, those details are divided by the time when each detail should be completed.

Shower Details

Name of guest of honor...

Cohost ....

Date of party ....

Time of party...

Location ....

Guests: couples or women only ....

Number of guests...

Theme..

Budget...

Guest is registered at which stores/Web sites.....

....

....

Menu..

....

Decorations...

Party Favors..

Games/crafts/other activities.................................

....

....

Devotions? If so, who will give them? ....

....

Guest list and phone numbers ....

....

....

....

....

....

....

....

Four Weeks before Party

O Make or buy invitations

O Put list of guests and their phone numbers near the phone; use to track RSVPs

O Send invitations

O Add the shower and guest of honor to your prayer list

O Plan party schedule

O Reserve place if needed

O Rent or arrange to borrow equipment such as chairs, tables, coffeemaker

O Line up assistants or divide work among cohosts:

    O Photography

    O Decorations

    O Food preparation

    O Person to record gift and name of giver as gifts are opened

    O Food and drink servers

○ Determine food service needs such as punch bowl and cups, plates, napkins, forks, coffee cups

○ Make shopping lists for food, paper goods, decorations, film, craft items, game needs

○ Find child care for any of your children not attending party

Three Weeks before Party

○ Purchase craft and activity materials

○ Purchase decorations

○ Purchase plates, napkins, cups, forks if needed

○ Decide what to wear; make sure it is cleaned, mended, and fits

Two Weeks before Party

○ Prepare any decorations that can be premade

○ If a craft is planned, test it now

○ Arrange to borrow any craft items needed

○ Gather items for games

○ Purchase nonperishable food items

○ Purchase gift and card; wrap and put away

One Week before Party

○ Call those who did not RSVP

○ Purchase any foods and party items still needed

○ Make food that can be frozen until party

○ Confirm reservation for location, rented items, etc.

○ Confirm assistants

○ Confirm child care

○ Plan schedule for party day, including all meals, party food preparation, getting kids to child care, last-minute cleaning, appointments, getting yourself ready

Two Days before Party

○ Clean public areas of house

○ Begin to decorate

○ Defrost frozen food in your refrigerator

○ Pick up items you're borrowing; keep a list of what belongs to whom

○ Chill drinks

One Day before Party

○ Finish decorating

○ Check to-do lists

○ Bake cake if you are making it

○ Pick up rented items

○ Make or buy ice

○ Buy fresh food and flowers

○ Prepare dinner ingredients to put into Crock-Pot next morning

○ Get good night's sleep

On Day of Party

○ Begin with good breakfast and quiet time

○ Follow your written schedule for the day or follow mine

  ○ Start Crock-Pot dinner

  ○ Finish decorating

  ○ Arrange party room, adding chairs if needed

  ○ Pick up bakery cake

  ○ Place your gift where other gifts will be collected

  ○ Put out camera, game materials, activity materials, and craft items

  ○ Set table

  ○ Do quick pickup of party area, all public areas

  ○ Wipe down bathrooms; put out extra toilet paper

  ○ Get children ready and off to sitters

  ○ Get yourself ready

- ○ Close the doors to rooms that are not for public viewing
- ○ Make beverages—punch, coffee, or tea can be started thirty minutes ahead
- ○ Have house, food, and yourself ready thirty minutes early and relax
- ○ Smile!

Day after Party

- ○ Thank God for all he did the day before
- ○ Put house back in order
- ○ Return rented items
- ○ Return borrowed items with thank-you notes
- ○ Get film developed
- ○ Write thank-you notes to those who assisted you
- ○ Add helpful information to your hospitality notebook if you have one

Bibliography

Cookbooks/Basic Entertaining

Better Homes and Gardens Cook Book. Better Homes and Gardens Books, Des Moines, Iowa: Meredith Corporation (any year, any edition).

Betty Crocker's Entertaining Basics. New York: Hungry Minds, 2001.

Martin, Judith. *Miss Manners' Guide to Domestic Tranquility.* New York: Crown Publishers, 1999.

Mills, Beverly, and Alicia Ross. *Desperation Entertaining.* New York: Workman Publishing, 2002.

Williamson, Suzanne. *Entertaining for Dummies.* New York: John Wiley & Sons, 1997.

Gift-Making

Cookies in a Jar and *Gift Mixes in a Jar* can be found in the Current USA, Inc. catalog and on their Web site: www.currentcatalog.com.

Gifts in a Jar series. (Titles include *Bars & Brownies; Holiday Fun; For Kids; Cocoas, Cappuccinos, Coffees & Teas; Soups*) G & R Publishing.

Ehman, Karen, Kelly Hovermale, and Trish Smith. *Homespun Gifts from the Heart.* Grand Rapids: Fleming H. Revell, 2003.

Oppenheimer, Betty. *Gifts for Herb Lovers.* Pownal, Vt.: Storey Books, 1997.

Before you head out to the bookstore, search the Internet. Key words that reaped results for my daughter as she assisted me with this book: birthday parties, family reunions, baby showers, wedding showers, dinner parties, recipes for crowds, entertaining, and tea parties.

Also check out your local library. They may not have the books I recommend but they may have others just as helpful. And they won't cost you a penny!

Visit
www.christianbookguides.com
for a discussion guide for *Heavenly Hospitality*
and other book group resources.

More Great Resources from Focus on the Family®

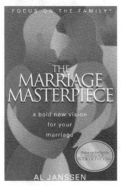

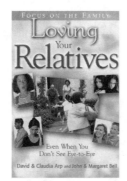

THE MARRIAGE MASTERPIECE

What ever happened to happily ever after? As divorce rates climb to all-time highs, many couples, including Christians, question the role of marriage and its "lifetime" commitment. In this book, Al Janssen looks at evidence of God's original intent for marriage, offers scriptural answers as to why marriage is still relevant, and paints a picture of what that means to couples today. Focus on the Family's marriage book of the year. Hardcover.

LOVING YOUR RELATIVES . . . EVEN WHEN YOU DON'T SEE EYE-TO-EYE

Family gatherings are often approached with dread, rather than as the connecting times they ought to be. Differences of opinion ranging from child-raising to holiday traditions surface and cause discord instead of harmony. This book is a practical resource with ideas to help build relationships of understanding and respect. Co-authors David and Claudia Arp and John and Margaret Bell offer multi-generational perspectives as they address sensitive issues with real-life examples and biblical wisdom. Hardcover.

HONEY, I'M HOME FOR GOOD!

When a husband retires or has decided to work from home, he's around 24 hours a day, seven days a week. It's a big adjustment for both husband and wife, and can often lead to friction. With humor and compassion, this book by Mary Ann Cook gives biblical advice for adjusting to the new situation. Check out the do's and don'ts, tips on balancing togetherness with each person's individuality, and ideas on establishing new routines for when husbands come home. Softcover.

Look for these books in your Christian bookstore or request a copy by calling 1-800-A-FAMILY (1-800-232-6459) or by visiting online at www.family.org. Friends in Canada may write Focus on the Family, P.O. Box 9800, Stn. Terminal, Vancouver, B.C. V6B 4G3, or call 1-800-661-9800.